Forever Broke

Get a grip on your finances and learn the money skills should've been taught in school

Tony Randhawa

1st Edition
ISBN: 9781794326965

Contents

Preface

English was never my favorite class in high school or university. In fact, it was my least favorite. If someone was to tell me that I would take it upon myself to write a book, or even just take the initiative to write something that wasn't required for a course, I would've said they were crazy. But here I find myself doing exactly that. It turns out writing isn't so dreadful after all.

My name is Antoni. You can call me Tony. Ever since high school I've been reading books on business and finance. I've traded currencies on my own for nearly six years and in 2016 I completed a finance degree. In addition, I've completed the Canadian Securities Course as well as a number of other "extra-curricular" finance courses you probably don't care about. I now work at a commercial real estate brokerage where my team and I sell commercial investment properties such as shopping centers, office buildings, and warehouses.

I'm no Warren Buffet but I believe I know enough to pass on a little knowledge in terms that teenagers and young adults will be able to understand.

I wrote this book to address one of the biggest issues with modern day education. The issue is that much of what students are taught in high school doesn't have any everyday application. The curriculum simply doesn't cover some of the most basic and relevant information a person needs to build and maintain a decent life in today's world.

For decades our education system has been churning out herds of financially illiterate graduates. If more people knew just the basics, the economy as a whole would be a lot healthier, but policy makers and curriculum developers are totally out of touch with the real world. I'm not saying that all high school education is garbage and you should drop out, I'm saying that knowing that the mitochondria is the powerhouse of the cell won't be of much use to you when you're planning your financial future and thinking about retirement. I don't discourage you from furthering your studies in areas you're truly passionate about. If it's of interest to you, then by all means pursue a career in it. Do what makes you happy, but don't turn a blind eye to educating yourself in areas like basic finance that have everyday implications on your life. Regardless of your passion, or your major in university, there are some things in life that you just need to know about, such as retirement saving, mortgages, investing, banking, credit... and the list goes on.

I graduated in 2012 from a high school that was regarded as "academic" and throughout my 3 years there, not a single mention was made of personal finance. It's almost as if they expect the money fairy to appear and bless you with the knowledge you need to succeed when you enter the real world. It was in grade 11 that I figured out that much of what I was learning in high school was not going to be of much help in the real world. If I had it my way, high schools would have a mandatory class that would teach what I am about to explain in this short book. For this reason I decided that I would educate myself on things that would be of use to me after high school and university. Everything related to personal finance can be learned from books or online, no degree required.

What you're about to read isn't going to make you an expert. It will, however, give you an introduction to much of the basics so that you can make sound financial decisions. It will help you develop a basic understanding of the world in terms of money. Hopefully, it will also spark some curiosity so that you will decide to study these topics further. I highly encourage this pursuit. It isn't a get rich quick scheme, it's a get rich slow and steady scheme.

What you'll need to get the most out of this book is an interest in learning about relevant real world topics that will affect you throughout your life (the interest is clearly there if you're reading this). Also you'll need to be able to think logically and understand some basic math. Those of you who have a math phobia, relax. It's pretty easy stuff, just putting numbers into formulas. While finance is a lot of math and statistics, I'm not here to cover that in depth. I've included just the basics so you'll see the odd formula or calculation here and there (mostly in the first couple of sections which I'd recommend not skipping). However, if you're interested more in terms of the math side of things then this book isn't for you.

There will be a lot of material covered here so don't expect to be able to memorize it all in one go. The idea is to give an overview and introduce you to the topics. Read each topic through and get a basic understanding, then reference it later. Like I said, this is an introduction. If you require more information than what is provided, then at least you will know what to look for when searching the web or looking for more advanced books.

If you've read this far you understand that it's up to you to take it upon yourself to gain the essential knowledge and skills in order to live a financially comfortable life. A large portion of society seems not to care about their finances. Actually, I shouldn't say they don't care about it. I think they just lack the initiative and are intimidated when they hear all the fancy words and acronyms such as equity, debt, mortgage, TFSA, RRIF etc... Or they just procrastinate and think that they'll figure it out when they're older. This is a bad way of thinking because time doesn't wait for anyone and you're only going to get older. START YOUNG. If you're reading this then that means you're on the right track!

Fun fact: did you know that when asked, "How have you planned for retirement?" one of the most common answers was that the respondents assumed they would win the lottery or inherit money when a family member passes away. That's insane! Ok, well, inheriting money isn't entirely uncommon. Regardless, that's still a pretty weak plan. Don't give yourself that excuse. Learn to spend less than you make so that you don't have to rely on your relatives' grim reaper to bail you out. But c'mon people, winning the lottery? Are you serious?! You have to be pretty delusional to think that the lottery is a safe bet for taking care of your future. If you think like that, then you probably won't ever be able to retire and you'll work till you die. That doesn't sound like fun. The bottom line is take control of your life and don't just "let things happen".

EDUCATE YOURSELF. PLAN. EXECUTE.

I'm glad I took the time to learn this stuff myself and I'm hoping that you, as the reader, will pick up a thing or two!

The Time Value of Money

Given that the majority of this book will be finance based, it is only appropriate that we start off with the basics. The time value of money and the mathematical phenomena of compounding underlie pretty much all financial theory and concepts. Let's begin with the time value of money. Essentially what the time value of money says is that $1 today is worth more than $1 tomorrow. The basis for this argument is that you could invest that $1 today so that tomorrow it is worth more than $1. Therefore, money is worth more the earlier it is received due to its potential to earn money. The methods by which you can invest that money will be discussed in later chapters, but for now just understand that if you're given the option between $1 today or $1 tomorrow you would rather take the $1 today.

$1 today > $1 tomorrow

This leads us into compounding. Let's assume we have $100 that we would like to invest. Let's also assume that we decide to invest our $100 in something that will pay us 10% on our investment per year. So that means one year from now we will have $110. Now let's assume a year has passed and we don't want to spend our $110. If we're able to invest that $110 at a rate of 10% per year for a second year we will have $121 by the end of the year. Again if we invest our $121 at 10% for a third year, we will have $133.10 by the end of that year. So clearly you can see a pattern here.

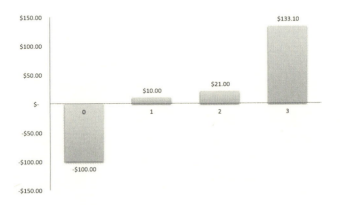

The bar chart above shows what would happen to your initial investment of $100 over the course of 3 years. The reason the X axis starts at 0 is because that is today, time zero. 1 is 1 year from now and so forth. You may also wonder why it is negative $100 at the beginning. This is because your investment (deposit in this case) is a cash outflow. You are giving your money to the bank, so therefore you no longer have $100 in your pocket. Then by the end of the first year you have made 10% on the $100 deposit and in the second year you've made another 10%, and finally at the end of the third year you decide to withdraw all of your money and have a grand total of $133.10.

The formula below is what is used to find the future value of an investment. In our previous example we started out with $100. That $100 is our present value (PV). We invested that $100 at 10% (r) for 3 years (t) and ended up with $133.10 (FV) by the end of the third year. Simply identify which numbers correspond to the correct variables in the formula and plug them in.

$$FV = PV \times (1 + r)^t$$
FV = Future Value
PV = Present Value
r = Interest Rate
t = Time

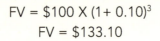

$$FV = \$100 \times (1 + 0.10)^3$$
$$FV = \$133.10$$

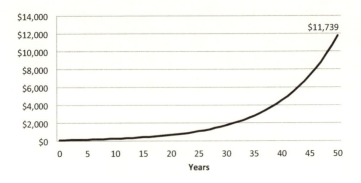

The graph above illustrates what the future value of your $100 invested at 10% per year would be within the timespan of 50 years. As you can see, the line of the graph is non linear (not straight), the line curves upward the more you move along the x-axis. Why does it do this? COMPOUNDING! This is the most powerful concept in finance and essentially what's happening is that you're earning money on the money you've earned from investing.

$$\$11,739.09 = 100 \times (1 + 0.10)^{50}$$

Just to reiterate, you can think about it like this; you start with $100 that you deposit in your bank and at a rate of return of 10%, you have $110 at the end of the year. If left untouched, that $110 will earn 10% the following year resulting in $121 by the end of the second year. So what happens is that the $10 in interest you earned on your $100 the first year is also going to earn 10%. The pattern continues for every successive year because your money is making money which is making more money. This is the power of compound interest!

Year 1: $100 + $10 = $110
Year 2: $110 + $11 = $121
Year 3: $121 + $12.10 = $133.10

So now if an investment manager says he can earn you 10% per year, if you let him manage your money, you can easily get a rough estimate of what he promises to make for you in a given time frame. By the way, be very skeptical if an investment manager promises that he can make you 10% per year on your investment. We'll get into that later on.

On the other hand, you may want to find out the present value of some amount at sometime in the future given an interest rate. In other words, what something in the future is worth today given a specific interest rate, or you could use this formula to figure out how much you need today, earning a certain interest rate, to arrive at a value in the future. A simple rearrangement of the formula presented earlier will yield the present value formula:

$$PV = FV / (1+r)^t$$

You would want to use the present value formula if you needed to figure out how much money you need to invest today to arrive at some future amount if you invest at r interest rate for t amount of time. For example, if you wanted to know how much money you would need to invest today at 8% to give you $750,000 in 35 years. Simply identify what number corresponds to what variable and plug it all into the formula to find the present value.

$$FV = \$750,000$$
$$R = 8\%$$
$$t = 35$$

$$PV = \$750,000 / (1 + 0.08)^{35}$$
$$PV = \$50,725.91$$

Interest Rates

There are two types of interest rates that we will discuss; APR and EAR.

Have you ever seen one of those car commercials that say "$5,000 down payment and 2.9% APR financing"? I'm sure you have even if you never noticed the "APR" part. APR stands for Annual Percentage Rate. EAR on the other hand, stands for Equivalent Annual Rate or Effective Annual Rate. Let's use a loan as an example. As I'm sure you all know, when you borrow money you pay the person or institution for lending you the money (otherwise there's no point for them to lend you money). The form of payment they receive in exchange for lending you the money is the interest rate they charge you. Effectively, you're going to be paying back more than you borrowed over the term of the loan.

Credit cards will usually advertise something like 22.9% APR, and in the small print it will say

0.06274% daily periodic rate. This rate is what you would pay on your credit card balance (it is highly recommended that you don't keep a high credit card balance). What this is essentially saying is that the interest compounds at a rate of 0.06274% per day. If we multiply 0.06274% by 365 days in a year we get 22.9%, which is the APR as previously stated. However, the mathematically correct way of expressing the effective interest rate that you'll actually be paying given the effects of compounding is 25.7% per year. The difference of 2.8% may not seem like a lot but take a look at the graph on the following page to see for yourself the difference between 22.9% and 25.7% compounded yearly over the course of 20 years on $100. Just remember that not all interest rates mean the same thing. It's important to make the distinction between EAR and APR.

Fortunately a financial calculator, Microsoft Excel, or one of the many tools on the internet can do these computations for you instead of typing them out manually in a standard calculator. I'm not even going to bother showing you the formulas for converting APRs to EARs and vice versa because if the previous section on the time value of money didn't put you to sleep then this would for sure. Knowing the math isn't important. Knowing the theory is.

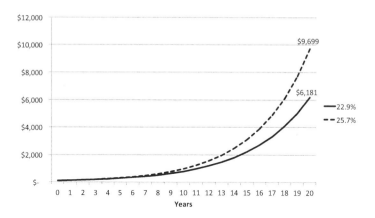

As you can see, that 2.8% has a fairly sizable effect after some time. By the end of 20 years, the difference between the two curves is approximately $3500! If you were to assume that the 22.9% is the effective rate you're actually paying, you'd be wrong!

The main difference between APR and EAR is that EAR incorporates the effect of compound interest where as APR does not. APR takes only simple interest into account. The official definition of APR is "The yearly interest payable on the amount borrowed plus any other applicable charges all expressed as an annual rate charge".[1] How can you tell the difference between an APR and an EAR? EARs are always quoted as annual rates. APRs, on the other hand, are usually quoted biannually, quarterly, monthly or some other fraction of the year. If it's an APR it will normally say so but always ask if you're unsure.

Clearly you can tell that it's good to know the difference between the two types of rates out there. Now you can impress your friends with your newly acquired knowledge of interest rates! ... Not.

Annuities

Yeah, okay, I know right now you're probably questioning your purchase of this book because up until this point it's just been a bunch of math. However, this math is the foundation of finance and it's good stuff to know in order to really grasp the concepts. Luckily for you, this will be the last section where you'll be introduced to new math.

An annuity is a series of cash flows. It can be thought of as a fixed series of payments you make, or are paid at a set frequency over a fixed period of time. There are two basic types of annuities: ordinary annuities, and annuities due.[4]

An ordinary annuity is when the payment is at the end of a period:

$$PV\ Ordinary\ Annuity = PMT \times \frac{1-(1+r)^{-t}}{r}$$

$$FV\ Ordinary\ Annuity = PMT \times \frac{(1+r)^t - 1}{r}$$

PMT = Payment at Each Interval

r = Interest Rate

t = Number of Payments

An annuity due is when the payment is at the beginning of the period:

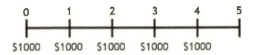

$$PV\,Annuity\ Due = PMT \times \frac{1-(1+r)^{-t}}{r} \times (1+r)$$

$$FV\,Annuity\ Due = PMT \times \frac{(1+r)^t - 1}{r} \times (1+r)$$

You'll notice that the formulas are nearly identical. The only difference is that the annuity due formulas are the ordinary annuity formulas multiplied buy (1 + r). This simply takes into account the extra compounding that occurs as a result of the payment being at the beginning of the period instead of at the end.

It's pretty easy to see the practical application of annuities. If you want to deposit $4,000 at the end of each year for 40 years for your retirement and you think you'll be able to earn a rate of return of 7% per year then you can easily plug those numbers into the FV ordinary annuity formula and find out how much you'll have in 40 years.

$$\$798,540 = \$4,000 \times \frac{(1 + 0.07)^{40} - 1}{0.07}$$

Or say you want to know what the present value of a stream of payments will be right now. Maybe you won one of those lotteries where they give you the option of a lump sum up front or that same amount broken in to separate yearly payments. Let's say this lottery will pay you $1M in yearly installments of $100,000 at the end of each year over the next 10 years (ordinary annuity). However, as a financially savvy person, you know that given the time value of money, that $1M broken into 10 payments over 10 years isn't the same as $1M given in a lump sum today. Let's say that a fair rate of return is 2% per year on super safe government bonds. We use this rate as our discount rate because it is a baseline for what we could potentially earn from investing.

$$\$898{,}258 = \$100{,}000 \times \frac{1 - (1 + 0.02)^{-10}}{0.02}$$

Pretty remarkable difference compared to the $1M up front. You can look at the $121,742 difference as the money you are leaving on the table by not going for the lump sum. For $121,742 you could put a significant down payment on a house, save for retirement, put your kids through school etc...

As we know, even a 2% discount rate can make a huge difference over time. So the next time you win the lottery, you're probably better off taking the cash up front instead of that amount spread over a number of years.

On a side note, the argument for going for the spread out payments is that you won't blow $1M in a short period. Maybe, if you're not a very responsible person when it comes to handling money, the $121,742 opportunity cost could be worth it. However, I don't know how to quantify a person's lack of money management skills so for the sake of this example let's assume you're disciplined enough to make the $1M go a long way. Or at least longer than a few exotic cars and a vacation to Hawaii.

For illustration purposes, the following result is what the yearly payments would have to be for it to make sense for you to accept the yearly payments given a 2% discount rate. All I did was rearrange the PV Ordinary Annuity formula to solve for PMT.

$$PV\ Ordinary\ Annuity = PMT \times \frac{1 - (1 + r)^{-t}}{r}$$

$$\frac{PV\ Ordinary\ Annuity}{\left(\frac{1 - (1 + r)^{-t}}{r}\right)} = PMT$$

$$\frac{\$1,000,000}{\left(\frac{1 - (1 + 0.02)^{-10}}{0.02}\right)} = \$111,326.53$$

Credit and Other Stuff

The credit card. It's nearly impossible to function in today's world without one. They allow you to shop without having to pay in cash or by cheque. They also allow the user to spend more than they currently have. It can be your best friend or your worst enemy. For many people it's one of the main reasons why they will never become wealthy. Psychologically speaking, it's a lot easier for a person to spend money with a credit card as opposed to physical cash. This is because when you pay for something with a credit card you're not physically handing over money in exchange for a good or service. In a sense, credit cards allow people to act wealthier than they are.[7] To limit spontaneous spending, it would be wise to withdraw physical cash in accordance with your budget, and leave your credit card at home so you can't spend more than you originally budgeted for.

A credit card gives its user credit. What does that mean? Basically the bank or credit company that issues you the card is giving you a revolving line of credit. Your card issuer is pretty much saying "Hey, I'll lend you up to $X per month to spend and then you have to pay me back at the end of the month (or whenever your bill is due) then I'll lend you up to $X again..." So if your credit card limit is $500 per month that means that the card issuer will lend you up to $500 each month so you can buy stuff. For instance, when you go out and buy those over-priced sneakers, you yourself are not directly paying Foot Locker. Instead, your credit issuer is, and now you owe the credit card issuer whatever the cost of the shoes is. Obviously you have to pay the credit issuer back each month on the due date, or you will be charged some ridiculously high interest rate on the money that you owe. Once you pay your credit card bill, you would think that you again would have access to the full amount of your limit. However, the bill has been calculated to a cutoff date in the month of billing. If at that cutoff date, you have not spent the full limit, then anything you have bought after that date is an amount that will be charged in the following billing period. This amount can seem nonexistent if you don't understand you're already spending toward a second billing date, and before the first bill is paid, you can find yourself at the limit very quickly. That's why we say it's a revolving line of credit; because once you pay your bill you get credit back for the amount you've paid. You also can't just walk into your bank and request a credit card with a $20,000 monthly limit unless you have a solid credit history. Usually they will start you off with a low limit like $1000 and as you build a credit history you will be able to increase your limit.

In case you didn't catch my point there, the costs of the purchases you make using the credit card are not taken directly out of your bank account when you buy something. Instead, that amount is drawn down from the credit limit that your credit card issuer is extending to you. On the due date of each month you have to pay back what you owe. This is how you build a good credit history.

Building good credit is very important for you especially when you're looking to take out a loan to purchase a home, car, or finance a business venture. Having good credit ensures you pay lower interest rates on borrowed money. Your credit score essentially is a number that represents how trustworthy/reliable you are if someone is to lend you money.

The interest you pay on a loan is a function of two factors. First, the probability that you will be able to pay the debt. Second, the amount the creditor will be able to recover if you become bankrupt.[16] If someone with good credit goes to a bank to get a loan they are much more likely to be approved than someone whose credit score is low.

Having good credit tells lenders that you are likely to pay back what you owe in the agreed upon time. When you look to purchase insurance, finance a car, rent an apartment, buy a house, or even get a job, credit checks will be run on you.

One great way to damage your credit is to fall behind on your credit card payments. Don't do that! Paying your credit card bill on time is very important in building a credit histor, especially as a young person. Some other factors that influence your credit score is how long you've had credit accounts open, how much of the available credit you use (try to use less than one third), how often you've applied for credit (too many applications looks bad), and what type of mix of credit you have (credit card, line of credit, mortgage, car loan etc.).[9] When you're young you likely won't have many obligations that require the use of credit, but you should start building your credit so that when you actually need it later on, you have an established history and a solid score which, as you know by now, will serve you well when it comes time to get a loan for purchasing a home.

Debit Cards

Debit cards are much simpler to understand than credit cards. When you use your debit card (aka your bank card) to make a purchase, the money you spend is taken directly out of your bank account, since the two are linked essentially the same way as a cheque book is to your chequing account. Another way to say this is that the money is debited immediately from your account. Debit cards will not affect your credit at all since the money you spend is taken directly from your bank account. Nobody is extending you credit so you're not on the hook to pay someone else back.

The main fee/risk associated with debit cards is overdraft. Your account will become overdrawn when you make a charge that exceeds the balance of your account, and if you have overdraft protection the purchase will go through, but you will be charged an overdraft fee plus interest on the overdrawn amount. However, if you have not opted for overdraft protection your card will be declined, and the transaction will not go through. Overdraft protection is always set at a certain amount that you cannot exceed. However, as a conscientious and responsible person, you should have no issue knowing the balance of your account so that you don't overdraw. Ideally, you have more than enough money in your account so that you don't have to worry about overdraft at all.

* * *

Comparing this to a credit card and you'll see how credit card debt can become a nightmare very quickly if you fail to pay your bills on time. Most monthly credit card bills list two amounts — minimum payment due and monthly balance. If you only make the minimum payment due, interest starts to build up (accrue is the fancy word) on the remaining balance at insanely high rates, usually in the neighborhood of 12% to 24%, in addition to late fees. Rates this high can royally screw you. Since this interest is compounded, it is very easy to get buried in a lot of debt. Financial advisors are unanimous in recommending that consumers repay their credit card debt first, before other loans due to the rate at which interest is charged and compounded.[10]

Coincidentally, at the time I was writing this section I happened to come across an article on Yahoo Finance that was written by someone talking about what they wish they knew before they got their first job after university. A quote from the author that caught my attention and that I thought was relevant to this section is the following description of credit cards, "I grew up thinking that credit cards were like a fountain I could dip into anytime I ran short on cash... I've learned there's only one way to use credit: charge what you can afford to pay off every month. Carrying a balance only wrecks your credit score and means you'll get hit with higher interest rates."[29]

The point of having these cards is so that you don't have to carry around cash or a checkbook in your pocket, and in the case of credit cards, if need be, you can pay for something before you have the money. But a caution here, you must know you will have the money to cover this purchase, and the rest of the credit card bill, when the next bill is due. The advantage of a debit card is that you can only spend the amount that is in your bank account, whereas with a credit card you can spend whatever the limit of the card is. The table on the next page nicely summarizes some of the key differences between debit and credit cards. Also, if you're interested in learning about some of the more complex mechanics of debit and credit cards, check out the link provided below the table on the next page.

	Credit Card	Debit Card
About	Credit cards are lines of credit. When you use a credit card, the issuer puts money toward the transaction. This is a loan you are expected to pay back in full (usually within 30 days), unless you want to be charged interest.	Any time you use a debit card to buy something, money is deducted from your account. With a debit card, you can really only spend the money you have available to you.
Connected To	Not required to be connected to a checking account.	Checking or Savings Account
Monthly Bills	Yes	No
Application Process	Somewhat difficult, depending on one's credit score and other details.	Easy, with basically no barrier to receiving a debit card.
Spending Limit	The credit limit set by the credit issuer. Limits increase or stay the same over time as a borrower's creditworthiness changes.	However much is in the bank account connected to the card.
Interest Charged	If a credit card bill is not paid in full, interest is charged on outstanding balance. The interest rate is usually very high.	No interest is charged because no money is borrowed.
Credit History	Responsible credit card usage and payment can improve one's credit rating. Credit cards typically report account activity to at least one of the three major credit bureaus on a monthly basis.	Does not affect credit history.

Source: http://www.diffen.com/difference/Credit_Card_vs_Debit_Card

Lines of Credit

A line of credit or LOC is basically a giant credit card with a lower interest rate and no travel points.[7] Essentially a financial institution agrees to lend its customer money up to some specified limit – similar to a credit card. However, a distinguishing feature of an LOC is that most of them do not have a defined repayment schedule meaning that, unlike a loan, you're not stuck with a fixed amount that you must pay at defined intervals. With an LOC you pay back "whenever" and usually only have to make interest payments every month – or some small fraction of the outstanding debt. Another key point about lines of credit is that they often use your home equity as collateral, meaning that if you don't ever pay back what you owe, the bank will take the equity you have in your home as repayment. Pause, you're probably wondering what "equity in your home" means. It will be discussed later on in more detail, but the easiest way to think about home equity is what the home is worth minus the outstanding mortgage balance. We'll also discuss mortgages in more detail later but they're basically a loan you take out in order to buy a home. Anyways, the benefit of having the LOC secured by your home equity is that this affords the borrower a low interest rate unlike some of the insane rates on credit cards. So, sounds like a good deal right? Borrow $100k on your LOC to buy a new BMW and only make low monthly interest payments. As the saying goes, "If it sounds too good to be true, it probably is."

A LOC definitely has some good features, but also some bad ones. The good features are that they allow you to borrow money at a competitive interest rate and also usually have no defined repayment schedule. The bad features are that they allow you to borrow money at a competitive interest rate and also usually have no defined repayment schedule. Why is this the case?... Human psychology; get some sort of reward now (instant gratification) by giving up something in the future. People are much more inclined to spend now without much thought of the future. Waiting is hard, and there is an innate desire to have what we want when we want it, which is usually without any delay.[22]

Because a LOC is like a huge credit card with significantly lower rates, it gives people the ability to be seriously financially irresponsible. It can be pretty tempting to make rash decisions and put a whole bunch of things you really don't need (or can't really afford) on the LOC so you can have those things now but pay for them later, maybe a lot later. My point here is that it can induce people to live beyond their means if they're not disciplined. LOCs have become increasingly popular in the past decade and there are all sorts of stories of people going nuts with them and piling up a mountain of debt that ultimately screws them over in the long run. Moral of the story... don't be one of those people. Be responsible and disciplined. Yes, I know, it's much easier said than done, but such is life. If you want to be successful in any capacity, you have to be disciplined.

Credit Scores

Credit scores were briefly mentioned earlier in the discussion of building credit but it's important that you have a basic understanding of how they work and what they mean. Canadian credit scores take into account 5 factors: payment history, outstanding debt, credit account history, recent inquiries, and types of credit. The scores range from 300-900. The US also has five factors that determine credit scores: payment history, amounts owed, length of credit history, types of credit in use, and new credit.[11] Very similar.

Credit scores above 800 are the best, 760 to

799 is good, the low 700s are fair, and below 699 is bad. Not only does a good credit score improve your chances of being approved for a loan or other grant of credit, it also helps you get the best interest rates and terms on the loans you're approved for.

Your credit score is only available for purchase online. You can check your credit score at the two credit bureau websites: Equifax and TransUnion. You are also entitled to one free credit report per year and it is highly recommended that you ask for it.

Let's quickly take a look at a real life example of when credit scores can make a huge difference. Let's say there are two people looking to buy a $23,000 car and finance it over a 66 month period. The only difference between the two people is their credit scores.

	Person A	Person B
Credit Score	830	599
Interest Rate	1.99%	14.99%
Payment	$368.22	$513.97
Total Interest Paid	$1,302.39	$10,921.44
Total Amount Paid	$24,302.39	$33,921.44

Person B pays **$9,619.05** more than Person A for the same car!

As we already know, the lower the interest rate the better. That means if you're Person A, you're paying far less over sticker price for the same car than Person B. Financing is how car dealerships make a large portion of their revenue. You'll sometimes see on used car dealer advertisements that they will approve anyone and everyone for financing regardless of their credit. What they don't tell you is that if you have low credit you're going to be paying stupidly high rates of interest.

Mortgages

Mortgage; a term you always hear people toss around in relation to real estate. So what exactly is a mortgage loan? It's a loan made by a financial institution, usually for the purposes of purchasing real estate.

So why do people get mortgage loans? Well for most people, a home is the most expensive thing they will ever purchase, and the majority of people don't have a couple hundred thousand dollars sitting in their bank account waiting to be spent. Therefore, they need to get a loan to be able to pay for a home because they can't afford to buy one outright.

Not just anybody can stroll into a bank and get a mortgage. Remember that bit about having good credit? Yeah... you're going to need that in order for the bank to trust you with a big loan.

There are 4 terms a person needs to know when dealing with mortgages. The first is down payment. A down payment is the money you initially put towards the purchase of a home. It comes from money you already have. You won't be able to get a mortgage unless you can foot some sort of down payment, usually a minimum of 5% of the purchase price of the home. So if you're saving up to purchase a $200,000 condo, you'll need to save up a minimum of $10,000 for the down payment. The second term you need to be conscious of is the interest rate/type. We've already discussed interest rates in a previous section. In the case of a loan, the interest rate is money you pay the lender as compensation for the money lent to you. The third term that you need to know is the amortization period. This is simply the time it will take to pay back the mortgage in full. The typical amortization period, depending on where you live, is about 25 years. The longer the amortization, the higher the interest costs. Total interest costs can be reduced by making additional lump sum payments when possible, and/or by arranging to make payments weekly or biweekly instead of once a month. The weekly or biweekly payments will each be smaller than the once a month payment. For example, for a $250,000 mortgage with a 5% interest rate and 25 year amortization, accelerated bi-weekly payments allow you to pay down your mortgage faster. You could pay off the mortgage in just over 21 years, and reduce your interest costs by almost $30,000.[8] Lastly, you should be conscious of the term of the mortgage. The term is the length of your current mortgage agreement. Terms can be anywhere from 6 months to 10 years. When the term is up, the balance you owe on the mortgage can be repaid, or you can renew the mortgage for another term. If you choose to renew, you have the ability to renegotiate your mortgage at the interest rate at that time, and choose the same or different options.

Types of Mortgages

High Ratio Mortgages

A high-ratio mortgage is a mortgage where the borrower contributes less than 20% of the value of the property as the down payment. The minimum payment is 5%. These types of mortgages are required to have mortgage protection insurance since they are riskier than conventional mortgages.

Open Mortgages

An open mortgage allows you the flexibility to repay the mortgage at any time without penalty. You may also choose, at any time, to renegotiate the mortgage. Open mortgages usually have shorter terms, but can include some variable rate/longer terms as well.[18] Interest rates on open mortgages are typically higher than on closed mortgages. An open mortgage can be a good choice if you plan to sell your home in the near future, or make large additional payments.

Closed Mortgages

A closed mortgage is a mortgage agreement that cannot be prepaid, renegotiated, or refinanced before maturity, except according to its terms. If you decide to pay off your mortgage before the mortgage term ends, or to pay an amount greater than your allowable prepayment, you may have to pay a prepayment penalty.[18] However, most lenders allow homeowners to make additional payments of a determined maximum amount without penalty. Typically, most people select closed mortgages.

Types of Interest Rates

Fixed Rate

The interest rate of a fixed rate mortgage is determined and locked in for the term of the mortgage. Lenders often offer different prepayment options allowing for quicker repayment of the mortgage, and for partial or full repayment of the mortgage. [18]

Variable Rate

These differ from a fixed rate in that with a variable rate, the interest rate you pay will fluctuate with the rate of the market. Usually, this will not change the overall amount of your mortgage payment, but rather will change the ratio of your monthly payment that goes towards interest costs and principal repayment. If interest rates go down, you end up repaying your mortgage faster. If they go up, more of the payment will go towards the interest and less towards repaying the principal. This option means you may have to be prepared to accept some risk and uncertainty.

For most people, a fixed rate mortgage seems to make the most sense. It gives you peace of mind knowing that your payments won't fluctuate. You know from the outset that you're able to manage the payments, and don't have to worry about interest rate fluctuations, because your payments will be unaffected. If rates drop significantly, then you can also consider refinancing your mortgage at the lower rate. This will result in some costs, but if rates drop a lot, and are likely to stay that way, then it may make sense to consider refinancing the mortgage.

How to calculate mortgage payments

Although you'll never have to do this by hand, the following will give you a clear understanding of how the mortgage is paid down and the relationship between the principal and interest portions of each payment.

Recall the Present Value Annuity Formula from a previous section. This formula can be used for mortgage calculations.

$$PV\ Ordinary\ Annuity = PMT \times \frac{1 - (1 + r)^{-t}}{r}$$

PV Annuity = Mortgage Loan Amount
PMT = Mortgage Payment
r = Interest Rate
n = Number of Payments

Let's say you're in the United States and looking to get a mortgage for a new home. You find the perfect home and it costs $562,500. Next you go to the bank and they qualify you for a $450,000 30 year mortgage at a stated nominal rate of 4% given that you're going to put a 20% down payment on the house. The question is: What is the monthly payment you'll have to make?

Alright, first off, I should explain a few things. Since the mortgage payments are monthly, not annually, there will be 360 of them in total. How did I arrive at 360? Simple...

$$30 \times 12 = 360$$
30 year mortgage
12 months in a year

Another thing to pay attention to is the quoted interest rate. A nominal rate is the face rate on a mortgage and does not account for the timing and periodicity of payments (APR). The rate we are given is therefore an APR. Since we are making monthly payments we need to adjust the rate accordingly to account for this. Recall the difference between EARs and APRs. Simply divide the quoted 4% by 12 and the result is 0.0033333333...

Once you have your numbers adjusted correctly, simply plug them into the formula. Note that you'll have to rearrange the above formula to calculate the payments. For those of you who may be confused, I have done it for you below.

$$\frac{PV\ Ordinary\ Annuity}{\left(\frac{1-(1+r)^{-t}}{r}\right)} = PMT$$

$$\frac{\$450,000}{\left(\frac{1-(1+0.0033\ldots)^{-360}}{0.0033\ldots}\right)} = \$2148.XX$$

Voila... now you've successfully calculated the amount you'll be paying each month! I know, this is incredibly exciting stuff.

If you'd rather just plug all the numbers into a formula without individually calculating the adjustments to the rate and number of periods you could use the formula below which is just a minor adjustment to the one previously provided. I have found from experience, that longer formulas can be a pain to type into a calculator all at once, so I prefer breaking things up as I did earlier.

$$\frac{PV\ Ordinary\ Annuity}{\left(\frac{1-\left(1+\frac{r}{n}\right)^{-t\times n}}{\frac{r}{n}}\right)} = PMT$$

PV Annuity = Mortgage Loan Amount
PMT = Mortgage Payment
r = Interest Rate
t = Amortization Period in Years
n = Number of Payments Per Year (12 in this case)

Unfortunately it is slightly more complicated to calculate the monthly payments for Canadians due to some seemingly pointless regulations in how interest rates on mortgages are quoted in Canada. US mortgages are quoted at a nominal rate with 12 compounding periods. Therefore, to find the monthly rate you pay you simply divide that quoted rate by 12. However, in Canada the brilliant decision makers decided that it made sense for rates on mortgages to be quoted with 2 compounding periods. So finding the monthly rate is not as straight forward as multiplying it by 6 and dividing by 12. The reason? Compounding.

Realistically, you probably won't have to do mortgage calculations by hand since there are numerous online tools that can do it for you quickly. The big takeaways from this section on mortgages are the key terms that you should know and understand, so that when you're prepared to purchase a home you can intelligently go about the process and understand what exactly it is that you're doing.

If you're interested in performing a quick mortgage calculation you can visit basically any major bank or mortgage broker website and they will have an interactive calculator built in. This will make life a lot easier.

* * *

We know already that a mortgage is simply a loan. We also know that in order to get this loan we have to pay interest. What hasn't been mentioned up until this point is the relationship between the interest and principal portions of each loan payment. The principal is simply the loan value.

What we calculated above, in the previous section, was the entire mortgage payment. However, I didn't mention that each payment consists of interest and principal. Interest is the money you pay on top of the value of the loan. The principal part of the payment is what goes towards paying down the balance of the loan. On the following page is what is referred to as an amortization schedule. It shows the breakdown of each payment. For simplicity I used a 2 year loan with monthly payments.

Interest Rate	5%
Years	2
Payments Per Year	12
Amount	$300,000.00

Payment Number	Payment	Principal	Interest	Balance
1	-$13,161.42	-$11,911.42	-$1,250.00	$288,088.58
2	-$13,161.42	-$11,961.05	-$1,200.37	$276,127.54
3	-$13,161.42	-$12,010.89	-$1,150.53	$264,116.65
4	-$13,161.42	-$12,060.93	-$1,100.49	$252,055.72
5	-$13,161.42	-$12,111.18	-$1,050.23	$239,944.53
6	-$13,161.42	-$12,161.65	-$999.77	$227,782.89
7	-$13,161.42	-$12,212.32	-$949.10	$215,570.56
8	-$13,161.42	-$12,263.21	-$898.21	$203,307.36
9	-$13,161.42	-$12,314.30	-$847.11	$190,993.06
10	-$13,161.42	-$12,365.61	-$795.80	$178,627.44
11	-$13,161.42	-$12,417.14	-$744.28	$166,210.31
12	-$13,161.42	-$12,468.87	-$692.54	$153,741.43
13	-$13,161.42	-$12,520.83	-$640.59	$141,220.61
14	-$13,161.42	-$12,573.00	-$588.42	$128,647.61
15	-$13,161.42	-$12,625.39	-$536.03	$116,022.22
16	-$13,161.42	-$12,677.99	-$483.43	$103,344.23
17	-$13,161.42	-$12,730.82	-$430.60	$90,613.42
18	-$13,161.42	-$12,783.86	-$377.56	$77,829.55
19	-$13,161.42	-$12,837.13	-$324.29	$64,992.43
20	-$13,161.42	-$12,890.62	-$270.80	$52,101.81
21	-$13,161.42	-$12,944.33	-$217.09	$39,157.49
22	-$13,161.42	-$12,998.26	-$163.16	$26,159.23
23	-$13,161.42	-$13,052.42	-$109.00	$13,106.81
24	-$13,161.42	-$13,106.81	-$54.61	$0.00

Pay attention to the interest and principal columns. You'll see that they have an inverse relationship. With each payment, the principal portion grows and the interest portion decreases until the final payment in which the balance of the loan is completely paid down.

Interest

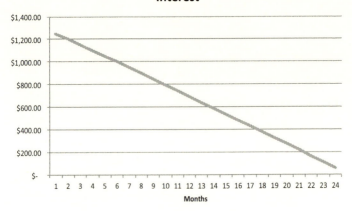

Principal

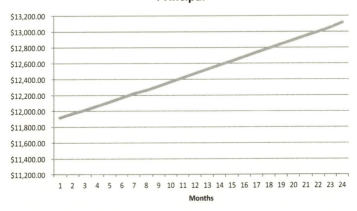

The Home Buying Process

Before you start looking at newspaper ads or the MLS, it's a good idea to figure out if you are ready to own a home and what you can afford. Figure out your financial readiness by calculating your monthly household expenses and monthly debt payments. Debt payments may include car loans/leases, lines of credit, credit cards, student loans... Add your monthly expenses and debt payments together to get your total monthly expenses.

Now you're ready to find out what you can reasonably afford. As a side note, you will want to plan ahead for the various expenses related to homeownership. In addition to purchasing the home, other significant expenses will include legal fees, home insurance, property taxes, utilities, home maintenance, and renovations.

There are a couple of rules that can assist you

in figuring out what you can reasonably afford given your total monthly expenses and income. You must understand these rules in order to evaluate if you will be able to get and maintain a mortgage – a good mortgage broker will be able to help you with this.

Rule numéro uno is that your monthly housing costs should not be greater than 32% of your gross monthly income. Gross monthly income is simply an individual's total personal income, before accounting for taxes or deductions. Housing costs include your monthly mortgage payments, property tax, and heating expense. Lenders add up your housing costs and figure out what percentage they are of your gross monthly income. This number is called your Gross Debt Service Ratio or GDS for short. To be considered for a mortgage, your GDS should be 32%, or less, of your gross household monthly income.

The second rule is that your entire monthly debt load should not be more than 40% of your gross monthly income. Your entire monthly debt load includes your housing costs plus all your other debt payments. This number is called your Total Debt Service (TDS) ratio.

The maximum home price that you can realistically afford depends on a number of factors. The most important factors are your gross household monthly income, your down payment and the mortgage interest rate. For many people, the hardest part of buying a home — especially their first one — is saving the necessary down payment.

The next step you should take is to get a copy of your credit report. As previously stated, your credit is a big deal! Before approving a mortgage, lenders will want to see how well you have paid your debts and bills in the past. To do this, they consider your credit history.

Before looking for a mortgage lender, get a copy of your own credit history. You're entitled to 1 free credit report per year. It would be wise to get it every year regardless if you're purchasing a home or not. Make sure to examine it to ensure that everything is accurate. You can ask the credit reporting agencies to correct any errors you find on your credit report. It may take some time to look into and resolve any errors, so check your report at least three months before you plan to start shopping around for a mortgage. If you do not have a good credit score, the mortgage lender could refuse to approve your mortgage, or may decide to approve you for a lower amount, and/or a higher interest rate. Some lenders may only consider your application if you have a large down payment, or if you have someone co-signing with you on the mortgage. Yes, I know this is like a broken record but you need to MAINTAIN GOOD CREDIT! PAY YOUR DEBTS ON TIME!

After looking over your credit report and ensuring there are no errors, the next step is to get pre-approved for a mortgage. A pre-approval is a preliminary discussion with a potential mortgage lender to find out the maximum amount they will lend you and at what interest rate. Before you even start the search to find your perfect home, it's wise to get pre-approved for a mortgage. This will save you a bunch of time because you will know what you're able to afford. This will dictate the scope of your search and expedite the whole process. Many realtors will ask if you've been approved before they start helping you so they don't waste your time, or theirs, by showing you homes that you can't afford. A lender will look at your finances and determine the size of the mortgage you can afford. Then the lender will give you a written confirmation, or certificate, for a fixed interest rate. This confirmation will be good for a specific period of time. However, be aware that a pre-approved mortgage is not a guarantee of being approved for the mortgage loan.[8] Keep in mind that the pre-approved amount is the maximum you could receive. It may be a good idea to look at homes in a lower price range so that your budget will not be stretched to the limit. Remember to include in your budget any additional costs you expect in the near future.

Now we get to the exciting part, enlisting the services of real estate agent and house shopping. Since you know how much you are pre-approved for, house shopping should be a breeze with the help of an agent. The perk of working with an agent if you're buying a house is that it doesn't cost you anything. The agent is paid on commission out of the pocket of the sellers of the home you decide to purchase. Another professional that you should hire is a real estate lawyer. They can look over all the paperwork and run some searches to ensure there are no outstanding taxes or debts (i.e. liens) on the property.

Once you've found the right house, you have to submit an offer through your agent. You may need to negotiate with the seller, but luckily that too goes through your agent. Once there is an agreed upon price, the house will go into escrow. This just means that the house will be held by a third party until the remaining steps in the home buying process are complete. The next step would be to get a home inspection, since purchase offers are normally contingent on the inspection to check for signs of structural damage or things that need to be fixed.

Inspections are voluntary but they're a good idea for obvious reasons. If the inspection reveals major issues, you can negotiate those repairs with the seller before you close the deal, or you could legally withdraw your offer. Your real estate agent usually will help you arrange to have the inspection done within a few days of your offer being accepted. This contingency protects you by giving you a chance to renegotiate your offer or withdraw it without penalty if the inspection reveals significant damage.[30]

Now you're ready to sit down with a mortgage broker to figure out the details of your mortgage loan. The mortgage broker's job is to shop different lenders to find you the best possible rate and mortgage that best fits your needs. Lenders will arrange for an appraiser to provide an independent estimate of the value of the house you are looking to buy.

Now onto finalizing the deal. This will include the final approval of your mortgage, and a meeting with your lawyer to finalize details like insurance and conditions, and the results of a title search.

Another wise step to take to ease the transition is to prepare for the move. There's a lot to do. Get your utilities and other services, like phone and internet set up, forward your mail to your new address, and hire a moving company. If you have been renting, you will need to give your landlord notice. A minimum of one month's notice is required. Preparing everything well in advance will help you make a smooth transition to your new home.

CLOSING DAY! The day you legally get possession of the house. Your lawyer completes all of the required paperwork. The home is now in your name, the payments are finalized, and you receive the deed and the keys.[31] BOOM! Done! That's it. Not too complicated right? Yeah, okay, it isn't the easiest process to work through but knowing how it all works will certainly help you out so you're not completely in the dark.

Fees and Costs to Consider

Mortgage Loan Insurance

Mortgage loan insurance helps protect lenders in the event that the person they lend to defaults, or in other words, doesn't hold up their end of the bargain and is unable to make payments. It enables people to purchase homes with a minimum down payment of 5% — with interest rates comparable to those with a 20% down payment. For example, if you want to put a 20% down payment on a $500,000 home that will work out to $100,000. By this logic, the larger your down payment, the smaller your mortgage loan will be.

The minimum down payment requirement for mortgage loan insurance depends on the purchase price of the home. For a purchase price of $500,000 or less, the minimum down payment is 5%. When the purchase price is above $500,000, the minimum down payment is 5% for the first $500,000 and 10% for the remaining portion. When you go over the million dollar mark things get interesting in terms of how much you'll be able to borrow and down payments etc. However I won't bother explaining that because chances are if you can or are thinking of buying a 7-figure home, you don't need to be reading this book.

The mortgage loan insurance premium is calculated as a percentage of the loan and is based on a number of factors such as the intended purpose of the property (owner occupied or rental), the type of loan (purchase/construction or refinance loan), and the size of your down payment. The higher the percentage of the total house value that you borrow, the higher percentage you will pay in insurance premiums. It's usually 0.60% – 3.15% of the loan value.

Deposit

The deposit is paid when you make an offer to purchase to show that you are a serious buyer. The deposit will form part of your down payment with the remainder owing at the time of closing. If for some reason you back out of the deal without having purchase conditions in place, such as financing, home inspection, etc., your deposit may not be refundable and you may be sued since it could be considered a breach of contract. The size of the deposit varies. Your realtor or lawyer can help you decide on the amount.

Appraisal Fee

Your mortgage lender may ask you to pay for a recognized appraisal in order to complete a mortgage loan. An appraisal is an estimate of the value of the home. The cost is usually between $250 and $350 and must be paid when you contract for this service.

Having an independent appraisal done on a property before you make an offer is a good idea. It will tell you what the property is worth and help ensure that you're not paying too much.

Home Inspection Fee

The Canadian Mortgage and Housing Corporation (CMHC) recommends that you make a home inspection a condition of your Offer to Purchase. A home inspection is done by a qualified home inspector to provide you with information on the condition of the home. Costs range depending on the age, size and complexity of the house and the condition that it is in. For example, it may be more costly to inspect a large, older, home, or one in relatively poor condition or that has many pre-existing problems or concerns. On average a home inspection should be around $200 – $500.

Survey

The mortgage lender may ask for an up-to-date survey or certificate of location. If the seller has a survey, but it is more than five years old, it will probably need to be updated. You should ask the seller to provide an updated survey, especially if there has been a new addition, deck or fence built close to the property line. If the seller does not have one, or does not agree to get one, you may have to pay for it yourself.

Remember, you must have permission from

the property owner before hiring a surveyor to go onto the property. Ask your realtor to help co-ordinate this with the owner. A survey or certificate of location can cost $1,000 to $2,000.

Title Insurance

Your lender or lawyer may suggest that you get title insurance. This will cover loss caused by defects of title to the property. The title of a property shows who the current owner of the property is and details such as outstanding debts connected to the property which, in most cases, you'd be on the hook for as the new property owner.

Land Transfer Tax

In some provinces and territories, you may have to pay this provincial or municipal charge when you close the sale. The cost is a percentage of the property's purchase price. Check online, or with your lawyer, to find out about the current rates. These fees can cost a few thousand dollars.

Property Insurance

The mortgage lender requires you to have

property insurance because your home is security for the mortgage. Meaning that in the event that you stop paying your mortgage the lender can take possession of the property. Property insurance covers the cost of replacing your home, and its contents, in case of loss. Property insurance must be in place on closing day. Typically this insurance will be $1,000 – $2,500 per year.

Moving Costs

This is pretty self-explanatory. Moving costs will usually be about $1,000 – $5,000. Or $0 if you do it yourself.

Legal Fees

Legal fees and related costs must be paid on closing day. The average cost is around $1500 (plus GST/HST). This includes administration fees and title searches.

Do you have to remember every single one of these fees? Absolutely not. Just know that there are a bunch of little extra costs here and that these will contribute to the amount you will have to pay for your home. Not every fee is listed here as there are some that are specific to certain provinces an situations. Just remember that the price at which the home is advertised isn't going to be the total amount you end up paying.

Checkout the following two websites for more detailed information:

https://www.cmhc-schl.gc.ca/en/co/buho/

http://www.fcacacfc.gc.ca/Eng/forConsumers/topics/ mortgages/Pages/Mortgage-Hypotheg.aspx

Rent vs. Buy

Okay, so we now know how to buy a home, but not everyone wants the responsibility of owning a home. Sure there's pride in ownership, but in all honesty, a home is a ton of work to maintain. Just ask your parents or friends that have their own home. This isn't to say that you don't have to work to maintain a rented property, but the burden you bear is much less.

People often ask the question, "Is it better to rent or buy?" It seems like a lot of people think that the answer is simple. Always buy because renting is a waste of money. However, the truth is that renting can sometimes be better than buying and vice versa. You don't want to make a big decision like this based on some over-simplified cliché. First off, renting is no more a waste of your money than buying apples from the store instead of buying a whole apple tree. You could just buy an apple tree and then get free apples forever, but you also have to put some effort into taking care of the tree. Or you could just go to the store to buy apples as you need them. Same goes for renting. Renting space is merely consumption of a good. You are paying to have a place to live.

It's always a case-by-case basis and there is never a definitive answer as to whether one is better than the other. The typical argument for buying instead of renting is that when you buy a home and get a mortgage, you build equity in your home with each mortgage payment, whereas if you rent you're simply paying the landlord's mortgage and "throwing money away". You're not just throwing your money away, you're getting a place to live that has no future value to you when you're done with it. As far as equity building goes, your mortgage payment doesn't all go towards equity, part of it goes toward building equity and the other part is interest. Don't forget about interest, taxes, and insurance.

A lot of young people just starting their careers can't afford a down payment, which means they either rent, or they stay with their parents until they can afford a down payment. Other times it's about convenience. No sense putting a down payment on a place to live if you know you're going to be moving to another city in the near future.

What most people don't understand is that

even when you buy a house you can still think of it as renting (assuming you get a mortgage). That might seem stupid to say, but hear me out. When you buy a house with a mortgage you're not renting space, you're renting money. The interest on your mortgage can be thought of as 'rent' on the borrowed money. The difference is that you're simply buying an asset (the home) that will hopefully appreciate. But what if your home doesn't appreciate? What happens if you bought a home right before a housing recession? If you have a $400,000 mortgage on a home that was valued at $500,000 when you bought it, but then is worth $450,000 when you want to sell it, that means YOU just lost $50,000. It doesn't matter what happens in the housing market, your mortgage will still be the same. Same goes if your home is valued at $550,000. You just made $50,000. The bank doesn't bear the burden of depreciation in your home value, and similarly, they don't enjoy any appreciation either. They just want you to pay them back what you owe plus interest.

The point I'm trying to make is that as the owner of a home you're exposed to fluctuations in the value of your home much the same as when you buy a stock and the price fluctuates. The bottom line is that everything is an investment and should be thought of in that context.

To answer the rent vs. buy question requires a combination of logic, reason, and a bit of math. If you only need a place to stay for a year because you'll be moving elsewhere, obviously renting is the better option. If you were to buy, live in the place, then sell it all within 1 year you'd likely have lost a lot of money due to all of the up front costs of purchasing a home. The home probably isn't going to increase enough in value over the course of 1 year to compensate you for all of your expenses. However, renting is quick and easy, and you can sign short-term rental agreements which make life a lot easier for those who plan to relocate in the near future. Alternatively, if you plan to stay in the same place for 40 years then it makes sense to buy because you get the full benefits of homeownership. Somewhere in this 1 - 40+ year range there is a crossover point where buying becomes more attractive than renting.

For this medium term time frame it's best to look at the rent vs. buy scenario in terms of opportunity cost. Opportunity cost is a term from economics that basically means the loss of a potential gain of something when something else is chosen instead. It doesn't even have to apply to money. You could say there is an opportunity cost in going to Taco Bell instead of going to the gym. You are forgoing the potential to burn calories and get in better shape to instead eat an unhealthy meal. However, in this case we're talking about money instead of tacos.

When thinking in terms of opportunity cost, the question becomes, do I want to tie up a bunch of my cash (down payment /mortgage payments) in a home, or could I find an alternative investment and rent instead? This opportunity cost, combined with the additional expenses of homeownership can sometimes negate the advantages that come with homeownership. Maybe you decide to invest your excess money you save from renting.

An argument for buying a home is that it's a method of forced saving. It might not be the economically most sensible way to save but it sure gives you an incentive. That incentive being that the bank will take back your house if you default on your mortgage payments. For some people, this is exactly the incentive they need in order to save money and build equity in an asset even though it might not make the most economical sense depending on a person's situation.

There's a link below this section that will send you to a webpage where you can download an Excel spreadsheet that will do all the rent vs. buy calculations for you. All you have to do is change the shaded input cells and everything else will automatically be calculated. You'll then be able to see a detailed cost comparison. A number of banks also have online calculators that do the same thing.

	A	B	C	D	E	F	G	H
1	Home purchase model							
4	Purchase price	250000						
5	Downpayment	50000						
6	Interest rate	5%						
7	Principal amortization (years)	25						
8	Property tax rate	1.25%						
9	Annual maintainance	1000						
10	Housing association dues (annual)	2000						
11	Annual insurance	1500						
12	Assumed annual appreciation	2%						
13	Assumed marginal income tax rate	30%						
14	General inflation	2%						
15	Monthly mortgage payment	1162.38	Assuming interest compounds monthly					
18	Cost of renting similar home	1500						
19	Assumed rental price inflation	2%						
20	Assumed annual (after tax) return on cash	5%						
23	Month	0	1	2	3	4	5	
25	Buying scenario							
27	Home Value	250,000	250,417	250,834	251,252	251,671	252,090	282
28	Debt	200,000	199,671	199,341	199,009	198,676	198,341	198
29	Equity in home	50,000	50,746	51,494	52,243	52,995	53,749	54,
31	Interest on debt		833	832	831	829	828	
32	Mortgage payment		1,162	1,162	1,162	1,162	1,162	1,
33	Paid principal		329	330	332	333	335	
35	Insurance payment		125	125	125	126	126	
36	Housing association dues		167	167	167	168	168	
37	Maintenance		83	83	84	84	84	
38	Property tax		260	261	261	262	262	
39	Income tax savings from interest deduction		326	326	326	327	327	
40	Total cash outflow in buying scenario		1,470	1,471	1,472	1,474	1,475	1,
42	Renting Scenario							
43	Cashflow that could be spent on home-purchase/expenses		1,470	1,471	1,472	1,474	1,475	1,
44	Rent	1,500	1,503	1,505	1,506	1,510	1,513	1,
47	Savings when renting	50,000	50,176	50,351	50,528	50,699	50,873	51,
50	Home value after 10 years	305,300						
51	Debt after 10 years	148,904						
52	Home Equity after 10 years	156,396						
53	Transaction costs of selling in year 10	18,318						
54	Net cash if home sold in 10 years (assuming no ca	138,078						
56	Savings after 10 years if renting	87,137						
58	Present value benefit of owning vs. renting for 10 y	98,197						

https://www.khanacademy.org/downloads

It really isn't all that complicated to understand. It will take the cost of home ownership i.e. mortgage payments, down-payment, maintenance, taxes, insurance... all that good stuff, and compare it to the cost of renting. Comparing the opportunity costs of both will yield a result that indicates which option makes more sense. This can be seen in the present value cell at the bottom of the spreadsheet.

Investing In Real Estate

Some sources say that as many as 90% of the worlds millionaires have made their money through real estate. Why is real estate the common denominator among millionaires? Leverage and cash-flow.

Real estate investors use leverage in the same way the average person uses it to purchase a home. Put part of the purchase price down and borrow the rest in the form of a mortgage. In effect, this allows the purchaser to buy the property for a fraction of the price.

The second part of the equation is cash-flow. If you or your family own the home you live in, it does not generate cash-flow. The way you get a property to cash-flow is to rent it out to someone who will pay you to occupy the property. This is critical because the rent payments from the tenant will cover your mortgage payment and ideally leave you with some money left over. This is what is referred to as a cash flowing property.

If you purchase a cash flowing property using leverage then this will magnify your return on investment. As you'll see in the flowing example, if you were to purchase a $2,000,000 property with a 30% down payment of $600,000 the return on your 600k investment would be significantly larger than if you were to purchase the property for $2,000,000 all cash. So what if you had $2,000,000 laying around to invest in a property? Should you go out and buy just one property all cash with all that money? Sure, you could do that but it wouldn't be the best use of your money since you could achieve a much higher return by using leverage to buy multiple properties or investing that $2,000,000 into a $6,000,000 property and borrowing the rest.

	A	B
Purchase Price	$2,000,000	$2,000,000
Down Payment	$2,000,000	$600,000
Yearly Mortgage Payments	$0	$56,000
Yearly Net Rental Income	$110,000	$110,000
Return	5.50%	9.00%

At a 9% return that means you as the property owner will get $110,000 - $56,000 = 54,000 ($54,000/$600,000 = 9.00%) per year in income!

$2,000,000 is not your average price for a

single family home so why did I use that amount in this example? Because $2,000,000 will get you a small apartment building, a 4-plex, a tri-plex or something of that nature. Single family homes don't usually make the best investments for long term cash flow purposes for one big reason; 9 times out of 10 you will only have one tenant if you rent out a single family home. This can be an issue because the goal of owning a rental property is to keep it occupied and generating money. A single family home will either be 100% occupied or 100% vacant. Its great if you can always have a tenant but once that tenant decides to leave then you will be left to foot the bill for the mortgage payments. The exception to this is if you convert the basement of the home into a second suite which you can rent out and thereby hedge against the situation in which your house is 100% vacant. This is why owning a multi-tenant property such as an apartment building is advantageous. Say you buy a small 6 unit apartment building. If 2 of the 6 units are vacant you still have an occupancy of 67% which is less than ideal but it sure beats 0%. At 67% most of the mortgage payment will likely be covered.

Income generation isn't everything though. The other huge benefit of owning investment properties is that your tenants are basically buying the property for you. Your down payment is your initial investment in the property and the remainder is the mortgage which will need to be paid down. Recall from the section on mortgages that part of the payment is interest which goes to the lender but part of the payment is also principle aka equity aka your ownership in the property. In 10 years you will have more than just your down payment as equity. You will have the accumulation of principle payments from the mortgage as well. In other words you will own more of the property in 10 years than you do when you initially purchased it. Add this to the fact that real estate typically appreciates at the rate of inflation.

Real estate investment isn't limited to residential properties either. Look around next time you drive to school or work. Every building you see is owned by someone or something. Everything from shopping malls, to industrial warehouses, to office towers, to apartment complexes. They're all owned by either wealthy private investors, pension funds, insurance companies, real estate investment trusts, real estate developers, syndicates, or the actual user of the property.

Real estate is everywhere. Train yourself to see it as an investment.

Types of Business Organizations

Before we talk about investing in stocks, I think it's good to understand how businesses can be organized under the legal system, so you can understand what a stock or share actually is.

The most basic form of business organizations is what is called a sole proprietorship. All you have to do to be considered a sole proprietorship is carry on business without adopting any of the other forms of business organization. If you mowed lawns as a kid, that is technically a sole proprietorship. The disadvantage is that you are liable for all debts, and all your personal assets are on the line if you get sued. If you hire someone to join your lawn mowing business you are solely responsible for all the work of that employee. If he ends up somehow destroying the customer's lawn then you, as the sole proprietor, are responsible.

The general partnership is very similar to the

sole proprietorship in that there is unlimited personal liability for the partners. This also means that partners are liable for each other in the ordinary course of business. If the partnership is sued then all your and your partner's assets are on the line. All that is needed to form a general partnership is for two people to carry on business together with a goal to profit. Notice how I said "goal to profit". This means that the partnership doesn't even have to be profitable in order for the partnership to come into existence. If you and your friend decided you want to start a car detailing business and you buy a pressure washer, wax, cloths, etc., even if you didn't make a penny, you still would have formed a partnership, as long as your goal was to make money.

A limited liability partnership is similar to a general partnership, except for the fact that in an LLP, individual partners are usually not personally liable for the wrongs committed by another partner in the ordinary course of business. Now you might be wondering why anyone who wanted to form a partnership would even consider a general partnership when an LLP is safer. The catch with LLPs is that not just anyone can form one. They are normally only for professional partnerships like lawyers and accountants.

Then there is the limited partnership. In a limited partnership there are two types of partners, General Partners (GP) and Limited Partners (LP). General partners have unlimited personal liability whereas Limited Partners have limited liability. The LP can only lose the money that they invested in the business. A common example of where limited partnerships are used is in real estate development. Say I want to build strip mall but I don't have the money required to do so. I'll need to find some people willing to invest with me. A limited partnership would benefit both my investors and me because I'll be able to run the project myself and they will be able to passively earn a return on their investment while at the same time limit their risk.

FINALLY, we get to corporations. Corporations are the most complex form of business organization. However, creating a corporation isn't all that difficult. There are a number of documents and some paperwork that need to be filled out and some fees that need to be paid. Anyway, the whole idea of a corporation is that when one is created it is considered a "separate legal entity", meaning that it can sue and be sued just like a person. Corporations also pay their own taxes.

Since corporations are considered separate legal entities, they must issue ownership stakes in the form of shares. The perk of being a shareholder is that you cannot lose more than your investment in a company's shares. A shareholder of a company has a claim on the residual value of the company after any creditors have been paid.[27] Basically, if the corporation has debts that it pays off, the left over money is distributed to the shareholders. In other words, their liability is limited. Unlike partnerships and sole proprietorships, corporations have what is called a board of directors. The people that sit on the board are responsible for the oversight and management of the corporation and they also are responsible for appointing what are often referred to as the C-suite managers of the company. C-suite refers to the CEO, CFO, CTO, CMO... you get the idea, the Chief _____ Officers. A company gets its directors though election by the shareholders.

You might be saying to yourself, "Well, since I am a shareholder of Facebook, can't I take a stroll over to Mark Zuckerberg's office and tell him how to run the company?" Being a shareholder of a public company does not mean you have a say in how the business is run. Instead, one vote per share to elect the board of directors at annual meetings is the extent to which you have a say in the company.[27]

Corporations can be public or private. There are some regulatory differences between the two, but the biggest difference is that the shares of public companies are tradable on exchanges. Public companies have thousands of shareholders. Private companies' shares, on the other hand, are not traded on exchanges and may only have a few shareholders. In fact there are far more private companies than there are public companies. The family-run bakery in your neighborhood might be a corporation and may only have a couple shareholders. Again, the main reason they would want to set the bakery up as a corporation as opposed to a partnership is to limit liability and reduce taxes.

Stocks

I'm sure that all of you have heard something like the following statements on the news channels or radio stations. "The Dow Jones Industrial average is up 200 points today" or "The S&P 500 is down 80 points." It wouldn't take a genius to surmise that an up day is good and a down day is not so good. But what are the reporters actually talking about?

They're talking about market indices. These are a measure of the performance of the markets. By tracking groups of investments, an index gives you a benchmark against which you can compare the performance of individual investments. If XYZ Inc. has lost 5% each year for the past 5 years but the index has gained 6% per year over that same period, it looks like XYZ Inc. is going through a rough patch or is underperforming relative to other companies in the index.

The words shares, stocks, and equities are synonymous. At the most basic level, a stock represents a share of ownership in a company. The more stock you own, the larger your share of the company is. As the partial owner of a company, that means that you theoretically have a partial claim to everything that the company owns after debt holders have been paid. In addition to this, you, as a shareholder, depending on what type of shares you own, may be able to receive dividends and vote. A dividend is just a sum of money, usually paid at regular intervals, by a company to its shareholders out of its profits. Not all companies pay dividends. It is up to the board of directors to decide to pay dividends or not.

A stock is represented by a stock certificate, which is a piece of paper that is proof of your ownership. However, nowadays when you purchase shares you won't actually get this document because your broker keeps these records electronically which makes the shares easier to trade.[27] You'll often hear about stock trading or buying and selling shares. This is all done via stock exchanges. The point of an exchange such as the NYSE or TSX is to keep trades centralized, and make it easy for buyers and sellers to exchange shares. Fortunately you don't have to go physically to the exchange to buy and sell shares. It can be done with the click of a button in the comfort of your own home.

The management of the company is supposed to increase the value of the firm for shareholders. If this doesn't happen, the shareholders can vote to have the management removed, at least in theory. In reality, individual investors don't own enough shares to have much influence on a company. It's really the heavy hitters like large institutional investors and billionaires, who have the power to make the decisions, since they usually will own a significant amount of shares, and therefore have more voting power.

For ordinary shareholders, not being able to manage the company isn't such a big deal. After all, the idea is that you don't want to have to work to make money, right? The importance of being a shareholder is that you are entitled to a portion of the company's profits and have a residual claim on its assets. Profits are sometimes paid out in the form of dividends, however the company is under no obligation to pay dividends. The more shares you own, the larger the portion of the profits you get. Your claim on assets is only relevant if a company goes bankrupt. In case of liquidation, you'll receive what's left after all the creditors have been paid.[27] Liquidation is when a company sells all of the things it owns (property, equipment, inventory) to pay back its debts. The importance of stock ownership is your claim on assets and earnings. Without this, the stock wouldn't be worth the paper it's printed on.

As previously stated, an extremely important feature of stock is its limited liability, which means that as an owner of a stock you are not personally liable for the company's obligations. As a shareholder you can't lose more than you invest. That still would suck, and does happen on occasion, but that sure beats losing your personal belongings. On the other hand, other company structures, such as sole proprietorships and partnerships, leave the sole proprietor or partners liable if the partnership is sued or the creditors come knocking.

There are two basic types of shares that most publicly traded companies have. Common shares, which have the right to vote, receive dividends, and receive remaining property if the corporation is liquidated. There are also Preferred shares that are entitled to receive fixed dividends on a regular basis, and a return of the amount invested before any payments are made to common shareholders. Preferred shares also typically do not have voting rights, and no claim on the residual value of the corporation beyond the amount invested. However, given that they receive fixed dividend payments at set intervals, and also get repaid before common shareholders in the event of a liquidation, they are less risky than common shares.

Why does a company issue stock to the

public? Why would the founders share the profits with thousands of people when they could keep profits for themselves? The reason is that companies sometimes need to raise money to fund expansion, company acquisitions, product development, and debt repayment. To do this, companies can either borrow money from somebody or raise money by selling part of the company, which is known as issuing stock. A company can also borrow by taking a loan from a bank or by issuing bonds. Both of the latter methods fit under the umbrella of debt financing. On the other hand, issuing stock is called equity financing. Issuing stock is advantageous for the company because it does not require the company to pay back the money or make interest payments, as would be required if it were to go the debt financing route. The first sale of a stock of a company to the public is called an initial public offering, or IPO for short. An IPO is done with the help of an Investment Bank.

It is important that you understand the distinction between a company financing through debt or financing through equity. When you buy a debt investment such as a high quality bond, you are almost guaranteed the return of the money you invested (the principal) along with promised interest payments. This isn't the case with an equity investment. By becoming a shareholder, you assume the risk of the company not being successful - just as a small business owner isn't guaranteed a return, neither is a shareholder. As a shareholder, your claim on assets is less than that of creditors. This means that if a company goes bankrupt and liquidates (sells all of its assets), you, as a shareholder, don't get any money until the banks and bondholders have been paid out. Shareholders are effectively the last to be repaid. Shareholders can earn a lot if a company is successful, but they also stand to lose their entire investment if the company isn't successful.

Risk

It must be emphasized that there are no guarantees when it comes to individual stocks. Some companies pay dividends, but many others do not. And there is no obligation to pay out dividends even for those firms that have traditionally given them. Without dividends, an investor can make money on a stock only through its appreciation in the open market. On the downside, any company can go bankrupt, in which case your investment is sometimes worth nothing. The market has its ups and its downs, but overall stocks have been a good long term investment.

Although risk might sound negative, there is also a bright side. Taking on greater risk demands a greater return on your investment. This is why stocks have historically outperformed other investments such as bonds or savings accounts. More risk translates into more reward potential. When it comes to investing, staying in your comfort zone is rarely profitable. If it was, then nobody would own risky investments.

"How many millionaires do you know who have become wealthy by investing in savings accounts? I rest my case."
- Robert G. Allen

Bonds

The bond market is massive. It's the biggest market in the world and arguably the most important. Without this market, there would not be liquid cash available for companies to grow, the economy to develop and the government to invest in.[25] Also, the interest rates in the bond market determine lending rates and discount rates around the world. The bond market doesn't get nearly as much media attention as the stock market and it's not really that exciting. However, the global bond market is said to be worth $100T. That "T" is not a typo. One Hundred Trillion Dollars!!! By comparison the world stock market is worth $65T. Bonds are a big deal, as you'll see on the next page.

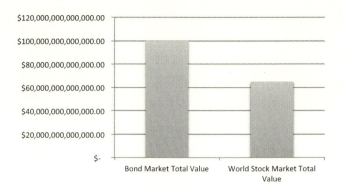

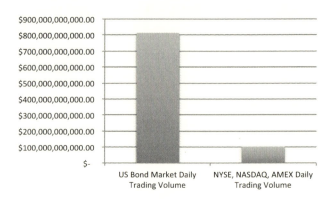

Plain and simple, a bond is essentially a loan. However, there's a slight twist; you play the role of the bank (aka the lender). How it works is that you loan your money to a company or government, they promise to pay you back with regular interest payments called coupons, and at the maturity of the bond, you will receive the face value (the principal amount invested). Bonds are not like stocks in that when you buy a bond you are not buying an ownership stake in the company or government that issues the bond. For example, a company may sell/issue bonds in order for it to raise money to finance a project, but by selling bonds they are not giving up equity in the company.

It is also important to note that the government bond market is the basis on which the financial system of every modern capitalist economy turns, because the interest rate at which the government is able to borrow is the most important figure in the economy. Every other financial asset is affected in some way by this rate.[15] If you pay attention to the news at all, this is why such a big deal is made about government interest rate changes.

Bonds are much less risky than stocks. And if you recall the risk/reward paradox i.e. more risk translates into more reward, and conversely less risk, less reward. The appeal of bonds is that they are much less risky than stocks (although not risk free), and most generate a steady stream of payments for you as the bondholder. Bonds and stocks typically move in opposite directions. For most people, the appeal of owning bonds is to mitigate losses during major stock market declines. This is why most people own both stocks and bonds in their portfolios.

Some of the risks of being a bondholder are quite similar to that of the risks banks face when lending money to someone. This risk comes primarily from the chance that whoever is borrowing the money defaults on their payments. Just like people, companies are given credit ratings that affect their ability to borrow. Therefore a company that has a low credit rating (risky) pays a higher interest rate on the bonds that they issue. The safest bonds you can get are Government Treasury Bonds also known as T-Bills. T-Bills are virtually risk free and thus pay a lower interest rate than bonds issued by a corporation.

As an investor you will want to consider a few factors when investing in bonds. Maturity refers to the specific future date when the principal amount that you have invested will be repaid, so ensuring that the maturity works with your investment time horizon is important. The interest rate (aka the coupon) is obviously another key component to consider. Bonds can pay fixed or floating interest (floating means that it will fluctuate during the life of the bond depending on market conditions). Bonds also don't pay interest in the same way. Some pay at the maturity of the bond and others pay in fixed intervals such as quarterly or biannually.

Face value or par value is the stated value of

the bond. Over the life of a bond, it can trade at a premium and/or discount to par value depending on market conditions. YTM, or Yield to Maturity, is the overall interest rate earned by an investor who buys the bond today at the market price, assuming that the bond will be held until maturity and the coupons will be reinvested. YTM is not the same thing as the interest or coupon rate that the bond pays. The current yield is the annual rate of return earned on a bond, and can be calculated simply by dividing the bond's interest payment by its purchase price. Therefore, if a bond is trading at a premium, one day and the next day it is trading at a discount, the current yield will also change. If you hold bonds outside of your RRSP (RRSPs are a later topic), you can be subject to capital gains and income tax.

Bonds can be bought and sold. If you buy a bond from the original issuer be it a government or corporation, you will buy the bond at par value and will be promised a specified interest rate/coupon. If you buy a bond that has already been resold prior to maturity you may purchase it at a premium or at a discount, or in other words, above or below par, respectively.

There are several agencies which rate bond quality and they all have a similar method of rating. Bonds are given a letter grade that corresponds to their credit risk. Below is a simple table summarizing the ratings and what they indicate. This is the format that most rating agencies follow, although you may find slight variations depending on where you look. Essentially the higher the letter and number of letters, the higher the quality of the bond, and the safer your investment is in theory.

S&P/Fitch	Moody's	Grade	Quality
AAA	Aaa	Investment	Highest Quality
AA	Aa		High Quality
A	A		Strong
BBB	Baa		Medium
BB	Ba	Junk	Speculative
B	B		
CCC	Caa		Highly Speculative
CC	Ca		
C	C		
D	C		In default

Bonds with longer maturities pay higher yields because you, as the bond-holder, want to be compensated for having your money tied up for a long period of time.

Central Bank interest rates have the largest impact on bond prices. As interest rates rise, bond prices fall. That's because when rates increase, new bonds are issued at higher rates, since the interest rates of the new bonds are based on the Central Bank Rate, making existing bonds with lower rates less valuable since they pay less. If interest rates fall, this makes previously issued bonds more attractive since they offer a higher return than what people expect given the current interest rates. These bonds would trade at a premium. Obviously you wouldn't be willing to pay the same amount for two things, one of which pays you 5% a year, and the other paying 2.5%, all else being equal.

If you hold onto your bond until maturity (think of it as the end of the loan period), it doesn't matter how much the price of the bond fluctuates. The interest rate you receive was set when you bought it, and when the term is up, you'll receive the face value (the money you initially invested) of the bond back as long as the issuer doesn't go bankrupt. But if you need to sell your bond before it matures, you could get less or more than your original investment depending on what interest rates are at that time.

This is a basic coverage of bonds. In practice they can be vastly more complex, but we won't get into that because as a regular person you likely will never need to know that stuff. Some terminology was left out on purpose because things can get pretty complicated. My goal here is not to turn you into a bond trader. My goal is to simply give you some foundational knowledge of these commonly used financial instruments. However, good bond traders can make boatloads of money. If I was somehow able to spark an interest, then I'd encourage you to learn more!

Inflation

Something that must be mentioned with regard to investment returns is inflation and the concept of purchasing power. Inflation is a general increase in the price of goods and services. It is measured as a percentage growth rate of price. Inflation reduces purchasing power, meaning that $1 today will not buy the same amount of goods and services as $1 a year from now. There is also something called deflation, which is the opposite, and also stagflation, hyperinflation... this isn't an economics textbook so I won't go into those. We will focus on inflation for our purposes here because North America is typically inflationary. The central banks of Canada and the US try to keep inflation around 2% per year by using monetary policy. Monetary policy is what the central bank does to control the supply of money and the interest rates in a country. However, the topic of monetary policy is far beyond the scope of this book. Just know that a good estimate of inflation is 2% per year and that too much inflation is bad, and high deflation is also bad. 2% seems to be where the central bankers are content (central bankers are the people who set inflation targets and manage interest rates). So if inflation is in fact 2%, and you keep $100 under your mattress, a year from now that $100 will buy 2% less stuff. Another way to say this is that you'll need $102 a year from now to purchase what $100 will get you now.

So what does this mean for our investments? Well, if our investment earns 9% per year we need to factor in the cost of inflation. Our net return after inflation is about 7% (9%-2%). As we know, and as we will see in further detail, 2% can make a huge difference. Especially when we're saving for retirement. This is due to the effects of compounding. Yes, it works both ways! Inflation is just like compound interest working against you.

So maybe you're thinking that you can fight inflation by keeping your money in your bank account. Let's use the analogy of a bucket filled with water. The bucket has a hole in the bottom so it leaks water. The size of that hole is the level of inflation and the water is the purchasing power of your money. In order to maintain a steady level of water in your bucket you will need to be pouring in as much as is escaping. The water you pour in is the interest you earn. Current interest rates on bank accounts are so low that there is only a drip going into your bucket. The water level of your bucket is declining almost as fast as the purchasing power of the money under your mattress. To illustrate this in further detail refer to the chart below where we assume we have $1,000,000 that we leave completely untouched for 20 years assuming a 2% rate of inflation.

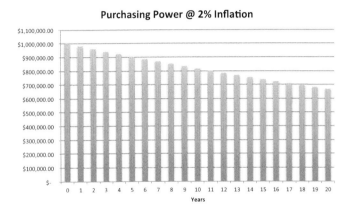

In 20 Years that $1,000,000 will only buy you $667,608 worth of stuff in today's dollars. You're not actually losing money, the value of the money you have is just decreasing. Your grandma's age-old wisdom of keeping the money under the mattress is false. Sorry, Grandma!

Cars

As someone who has loved cars since a young age, this is difficult to admit; cars are awful. Vehicles are probably the single worst expenditure a person can make. Why? Because they depreciate ridiculously fast, with the exception of rare old or limited production high-end cars. However, we're not talking about 1960s Ferraris, we're talking about regular vehicles that you see on the road. According to CarFax, the minute you drive a new car off the lot it loses approximately 10% of its value and by the end of the first year it will have lost an additional 10% on average. But this number is not fixed. Cars with less brand-name appeal and fewer options can be hit harder, depreciating as much as 50% in some cases. So when you buy a car that's less than two years old, be sure to know how much it has decreased in value. And don't be fooled into thinking depreciation slows after the first year. New cars continue to lose value rapidly for 4 more years, averaging a decline of 15% - 25% per year. On average, a new car will lose 60% of its total value over the first five years of its life and will continue to deprecate at a slower rate thereafter. So if you purchase a new $50,000 vehicle, it will be worth roughly $20,000 after 5 years assuming a regular amount of driving and wear. Let me rephrase this; if you make an investment where you turn $50,000 into $20,000, is that a good investment?

Therefore, just in depreciation alone, you've lost $30,000. But we're not done yet. Cars also need to be insured. Insurance on new vehicles is guaranteed to be more expensive than a comparable older model. Oh and lets not forget maintenance. Cars have lots of moving parts, and those moving parts need to be maintained and replaced as they are used. Fluid changes, brakes, tires, spark plugs, batteries, etc...

But you know what's worse than driving and maintaining a rapidly depreciating car?... car loans. Unlike getting a loan to purchase property, which is very likely to, at minimum, maintain its value and even produce cash flow if it's an investment, cars are guaranteed to cost you money and guaranteed to lose value. Paying interest on a loan to purchase something that is guaranteed to go down in value makes no sense. When I tell people this the common response is, "Well I can't afford to buy my $40,000 vehicle in cash" – Precisely, you can't afford it. If you can't buy your car all cash then you probably shouldn't be driving it. The only caveat to this is if you have an investment opportunity that will earn you a greater percentage return than the interest rate on your auto loan OR you can somehow get a 0% loan, which is highly unlikely seeing as how most lenders will lend to you at 4% if you have great credit and north of 10% if you have bad credit. At the time of writing, interest rates are expected to increase in the near future which means that auto loans will only become more expensive. Auto loans have also been increasing in their average term length for over a decade. Longer terms also mean higher interest rates. People are digging themselves into deep holes just to be able to drive a new vehicle.

With the increasing terms and higher interest rates, many people find themselves with what is called "negative equity" in the vehicle, meaning you owe more on it than it's worth due to depreciation. This situation is also known as being "upside down". If you make a down payment that's too small, you put yourself further underwater. And you go deeper still the longer the loan term. This means that it will COST YOU MONEY TO SELL YOUR CAR. What a shitty situation to be in!

The time it takes you to build equity in the car depends on what you bought and your down payment. And equity is what you want because it gives you choices. When you have equity in the car, you can sell it if your other bills get out of hand or you lose your job. Negative equity, on the other hand, limits your options if you're in a money bind. It also ties you down if you get tired of your car before it's paid off. A buyer will only pay you what the car is worth, not what you owe on it. You're stuck with the balance of the loan.

The average person keeps their car for 6-7 years. It also happens that the average loan nowadays is 6-7 years. This means that people basically finance a new car, pay off the loan including all of the interest and then sell the car right when they've paid it off and lose upwards of 60% of the value of the car. If you don't think that sounds nuts then please re-read the chapter.

This is a great segway into the automotive cardinal sin: leasing. For somebody on a budget, it's easy to see why leases are so tempting: You get a brand new car and a monthly payment that's lower than a car loan payment. But leases are a devil in disguise.

To help understand why leasing a vehicle is

the most expensive way to drive a vehicle, lets look at it from the dealers perspective. If you're a BMW dealer and you lease someone a car for $50,000 and in 5 years they return that car to you and it's worth $20,000, in order to keep from losing that $30,000 difference, you'd have to lease the car out so that the sum of the lease payments to you is more than $30,000. And because you're a dealer and you need to make money, at minimum you need to cover what it goes down in value. Also, since you're a car company, you know that you make more money on the interest payments via financing and leasing a car than you do from the profit of selling a car. Therefore, you're going to want to make sure the lease payments you receive cover the depreciation of the vehicle you're leasing out, give you a profit on top, AND pay you interest! So as the consumer, (the person leasing the car) in your monthly lease payment, you're paying the depreciation of the car, the dealers' profit, as well as interest! Oh, and that's not all. Leases have mileage limits where you're penalized if you drive over a set amount. These penalties can range from 5 to 20 cents a kilometer. What's more, a lease allows for normal wear to the car, but if the dealership considers vehicle to have wear and tear above what they define as normal at the end of the lease, they can charge you extra. Not to mention, insurance is more on leases. There is no mathematical way that, on average, leasing a car is cheaper than owning a car. Car dealers are in the business of making money, and there's no such thing as a poor car dealer. They know the math a lot better than you do.

There are some exceptions for business owners or others who can deduct certain vehicle costs where it actually works out that it's better to lease. However, I've assumed for simplicity that most people reading this can't write off lease payments.

So yeah, cars suck. There's really no way to drive a car that doesn't have a downside. For those who live in big cities, driving a car doesn't even make sense. For everyone else, the best way to drive a vehicle is to buy a used one all cash. Sure, financing a used car is much better than financing a new one assuming the used car in question has taken the better part of its depreciation hit, but the interest rates on used cars are always higher than on new cars. The best option is to just buy a used car you can afford to pay for upfront.

There are many advantages to buying used. First, you get more car for your money. A new base Toyota Camry is probably $36,000. A 7 year old comparable model Lexus is about $18,000. You're not making any monthly payments on the Lexus, and in 5 years the Lexus might be worth $10,000 and the Camry is worth $14,000. Cars made in the past 10 years also don't show their age as much as cars made in the 1990s and early 2000s. Many cars made 10 years ago could still easily be mistaken for new cars.

Something to keep in mind is that not all cars are made equal. Some are far more reliable and therefore cheaper to own than others. If I was in the market for a used car right now I would stay away from most, but not all, European and American cars. Do your research and find the common issues, cost of parts, and reliability of the vehicles that interest you most. I like to go on AutoTrader and Kijiji and search for the cheapest and highest mileage cars for sale of the particular make and model I'm interested in to get an idea of what sort of issues to look out for and also to see how many are for sale. If I see lots of the same vehicle for sale that have super high mileage then I'm pretty confident that it's a good vehicle. Unreliable and poorly made vehicles rarely make it that far before going to the junkyard. You won't find many BMWs and Fiats with 400,000+ kms for sale - they don't exist.

This brings me to my next point; much of the engineering and tech in new cars is fairly pioneering and unproven. What I mean by this is that lots of carmakers are trying to reinvent the wheel. They're adding unnecessary complication to something that doesn't need it. More gadgets and advanced tech equals more stuff that can break. Others take a more "if it ain't broke, don't fix it" approach and simply refine something that has proven itself to be solid. An example of this is Toyota/Lexus. The engine in the 2019 4Runner is essentially the same engine used in the 2003 version. Sure, over the years they've made some tweaks here and there but it's basically the same thing. And guess what... they last a very long time and are inexpensive to maintain. Let the manufacturer work out the kinks before you sink thousands of dollars into a vehicle.

So the moral of the story is that buying, financing, or leasing a new car is bad for your bank account. Do your research and buy a solid used car with cash. Buying new cars is the one surefire way to remain in the middle class.

Personal Finance and Investment Management

Let's talk retail banking. Most people go to their local bank branch to get advice about investing assuming that the people at the bank actually know what they're talking about. The reality is that most people that work at your local bank branch don't know much more than you do. They're just salespeople. Anyone can work in retail banking. Literally anyone. You don't need a degree in finance or economics.

The people at the bank are put through short training programs. These training programs are provided by their particular bank, so they can do their jobs and ultimately make the bank money. The majority of this training is sales training. This isn't to say that the employees don't take it upon themselves to get educated beyond what's expected, but don't think that the person at the bank always knows what's best just because they work there. The reality is that their job is to make the bank money by selling the bank's products (GICs, Mutual Funds, Cards, Annuities etc.).

They're all salespeople just like the guy at Best Buy trying to sell you a home theater system with extended warranty. They have sales targets they have to meet and their pay structure has a lot to do with commissions and "points systems" that go towards sales targets that are used to evaluate their performance. Like most sales people, there is a lot of pressure to upsell regardless if the customer will get any value or not. Whenever they sign you up for a checking account, or a line of credit, or whatever else they push, they're being rewarded. After all, it's called "retail" banking for a reason. Don't take everything that these people say as gospel.

I have nothing against people who work in retail banking. They're just ordinary people trying to make a living. However, you can't expect someone to always act in your best interest when they're incentivized by commissions.

When you talk to anyone at a bank or financial institution that's trying to tell you what to do with your money, you should ask that person whether or not he/she is a fiduciary. A fiduciary is someone who is obligated to act in your best interest, and not put their own interests above yours.

An example of this is a real estate agent. Real estate agents are obligated to get you the best price for your home. They can't attempt to close the deal as quickly as possible with no regard for the price they get for you, just so that they can make a quick commission. Similarly with finance professionals, if they aren't a fiduciary they're not obligated to act in your best interests. If they say they're not a fiduciary then be skeptical of everything they say no matter how "great" it may sound. A study conducted by the Harvard Business School concluded that between the years of 1996 – 2002, average returns of funds recommended by advisors earned 2.9% per year (excluding up front charges) – compared to 6.6% earned by investors who took charge of their own affairs.[3]

You're probably thinking that I'm some "smart ass" that thinks he knows it all, but I'm not. I'm simply speaking the truth. I known plenty of people that have worked in retail banking that would completely agree with me. There are also numerous articles online that shine light onto the issue of sales in banking.

Be prepared and be educated. It's your money and your responsibility. Don't let someone pressure you into doing something you're unsure of just so they can meet their sales quota.

Investment Managers

A lot of investment managers will promise that they will get you 8% per year on the money you give to them to manage. 8% per year sounds pretty good, right?

Yes, that's a solid return each year... if you actually get 8%. Sadly, that's not the reality that most people face. For starters, the investment manager probably forgot to mention their 2% per year management fee that will be charged whether they make you a dime or not. So now we're down to 6% ... a far cry from 8% when you take compounding into consideration. Take a look at the difference that the 2% fee makes on a simple one-time investment of $10,000 over the course of 30 years. It's pretty remarkable.

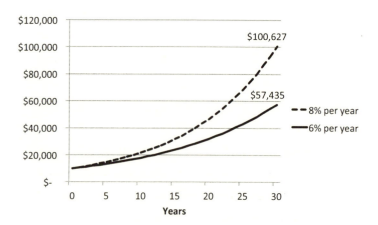

By the end of year 30, the 8% per year return on the $10,000 has nearly doubled that of the 6% per year return. Did you catch that? NEARLY DOUBLE! That's just from a 2% difference in the rate of return you are earning. You get the idea.

So where does this leave you as the client? ... well, earning 6% per year. But not exactly. Something that people fail to realize is that rarely will you actually get 6% per year or even 8% on a consistent basis. As everyone should know, the market goes though cycles, and whatever yearly return you are promised is simply an average of what you are expected to receive over a set period of time in the future. So one year you may lose money and the next you may make money, but the fact is that when you're investing, no matter how you do it, you're going to have to deal psychologically with the ups and downs of the market. The growth of your investments will likely not be smooth like the chart provided above.

The 2% management fee isn't the only fee you'll incur. Almost always, a bunch of other little fees are tacked on that will eat away at your returns. They're small but they add up. Over the course of a few decades these fees will eat up a significant portion of your hard earned and invested money. Be sure to pay particular interest to these additional fees.

To justify giving your money to an investment manager, he/she will have to outsmart and outperform the market by the cost of the management fees. 2% might not seem like much, but it's a lot easier said than done to consistently beat the market year after year by a margin of 2%, as you'll find out later.

Diversification

When you hear people talk about diversifying their portfolio they usually say, "Don't put all your eggs in one basket." If you put all your eggs in one basket, and if you drop the basket, you'll be making scrambled eggs. Similarly with investing, you don't want to put all your money into one investment, because if that company tanks, then you're out of luck and have lost a significant portion of your investment. This is why everyone in finance talks about diversification.

By diversifying you're reducing risk. For example, say you have a portfolio of 10 stocks, and your buddy has a portfolio consisting of only 2 of the 10 stocks you have. If 1 of those 2 stocks goes to $0, then you've lost 10% of your portfolio, whereas your buddy has lost 50%! The flip side is that if that stock goes on a massive rally and doubles within a day, then your buddy has seen a far larger appreciation in his portfolio than you. However, the key to successful investing is knowing how to manage risk and preserve capital. As a matter of principle, you should be more conscious of your downside risk than your upside potential.

In the movie The Wolf of Wall Street, Leonardo Dicaprio's character started off as a penny-stockbroker. He called people up and tried to sell them on the hottest stock that had "huge upside potential", and he of course got a commission for selling the stocks. The suckers that ended up buying from him were too caught up in the sales pitch to even consider the downside risk of the investment. As a result, a lot of people lost a lot of money. Some decided to risk everything, from their retirement savings to education funds for their kids, in the hope that they would be able to double their money. That's not investing. That's gambling.

If the companies that Leo and his stock brokers were pushing were so amazing and had so much upside potential, and such low downside risk, why on earth would these brokers have wanted to sell the shares to clients? Why didn't they just buy up all the shares for themselves and make millions? But that's not the way it works. They needed clients in order to get commissions, because the stocks they were pushing were not all that they were cracked up to be and the brokers knew it. Although Leo, as the smooth talking broker was also to blame, a lot of the people that bought from him clearly didn't know much about money and finance, and got too emotionally attached to the idea of seeing double, if not triple digit returns. Another rant... my bad. But you get the idea. Do your homework.

Diversification is not as simple as randomly selecting a bunch of companies and purchasing their shares. There needs to be some thought that goes into it. Just think about what the word "diverse" means. "Showing a great deal of variety; very different" – that's straight from the dictionary. So when thinking about diversification in an investment context, don't just think different stocks. Think about the type of industries that the companies are in, and even different types of investments altogether, such as bonds, commodities, REITs, real estate etc.. If you had invested a bunch of money into 20 stocks that are all in the Oil and Gas industry then your portfolio in 2015/2016 wouldn't be looking too great. This is because the factors that affect different companies in the same industry are all very similar if not the same. On the other hand you don't want to be over-diversified because then you'll never make any money because your money will be spread too thin. If you only have a few thousand dollars, put it in one or two investments.

Back in the early 2000s the whole tech industry imploded. Everyone thought that every .com had huge potential so they invested a lot of money in them even though there was no fundamental basis for doing so. Then shit hit the fan, and lots of people lost a lot of money. However, at this same time, if you had a well diversified portfolio, including investments in bonds, commodities and REITs, that would have helped offset the losses, because the factors that effect the price of REITs, bonds, commodities are not all going to be the same, and thus they won't move in lock-step. Or in other words, they're not as highly correlated as two stocks in the same industry.

You're probably wondering what a REIT is. REIT stands for Real Estate Investment Trust. They're similar to mutual funds in that you buy shares in the fund, but instead of owning company shares or bonds, the REIT owns income producing real estate. This allows both small and large investors to invest in various forms of real estate from apartment complexes, to shopping malls, to office buildings without actually purchasing the properties themselves yet still participate in the cash flows the properties generate in the form of monthly or quarterly dividend payments

* * *

Something else that needs to be addressed here is the difference between passive and active management. Passive management means that you're not frequently buying and selling investments in your portfolio, whereas active is the opposite. I'm not aware of any well-known financial expert that would recommend that average people actively manage their investments. Frequent trading results in more transaction costs being incurred. Lots of brokerages charge fairly cheap commissions compared to a decade ago, but unless you have a decent sized portfolio, those commission charges will add up fast if you think you're going to beat the market by trading frequently. In fact, according to The Little Book of Common Sense Investing, over one year, 29% of active managers on average, would be expected to outpace the S&P 500 index, over five years about 15% would be expected to win; over 10 years, 9%; over 25 years, 5%; and over 50 years just 2% of active managers would be expected to win... The odds are not in the favor of the active manager.[3]

People tend to think there is a bonus for

activity in investing, when there most certainly is not. Fighting this tendency can result in a big payoff because there is a penalty for being overactive due to the associated fees and expenses.[13]

"The stock market is designed to transfer money from the active to the patient"
- Warren Buffett

A key lesson in finance, especially investment management and trading, is to not get cocky and think you can outsmart the market. The reality is that some of the smartest people in the world work in finance and put in 80+ hours a week to get an edge on the rest of the market. Wall Street employs Ivy League grads and math and physics PHDs to run their trading shops and investment firms. You think you can beat them? Well, good luck, because they're the ones you're competing against. Oftentimes they don't even produce good returns. In fact a lot of them don't even beat the market consistently.

By actively managing your investments you may have your moments, but I guarantee that your long run performance will not be favorable. It's human nature to try to pick the right horse to win the race, but investing shouldn't be thought of as a game. As for me, I'll be happy earning the market return because I'd rather do other things with my time than try to beat the market at its own game.

Oh, and remember our friends who are "professional active managers"? There are studies that show that monkeys and house cats have just as good stock picking abilities as the "pros".

Yes, there are some that are gifted traders and stock pickers, but those people are few and far between. Don't think that they always beat the market either.

One thing you have to be aware of and have to learn is how to deal with down turns in the market. The market doesn't move up consistently day after day. There will be periods when the market declines. How you deal with down turns or recessions will have a big impact on your long term investing success. A lot of people buy high and sell low. History shows that it's best to sit on your hands and ride out the rough patches. Trying to time the market or frantically buying and selling won't get you very far.

"Unsuccessful investors are dominated by emotion. Rather than responding coolly and rationally to market fluctuations, they respond emotionally with greed and fear"
- Seth Klarman

Mutual Funds & Index Funds

Mutual funds have been mentioned a couple times, but we haven't gotten into what they actually are. A mutual fund is a pool of "professionally" managed money. This pool of money is made up of many investors that have handed their money over to the fund to receive "professional management" and diversification. Mutual funds make diversification easy and cheap. You don't even need to open up a trading account to purchase shares of a mutual fund as this can be done through your bank.

For an individual person to construct a well diversified portfolio would take a lot of time, research, and expertise. There's a lot of work that goes into it. This is why mutual funds are so appealing. You just have to buy shares in the fund and you automatically have a pro rata share of all of the assets that the fund owns. Pro rata share just means a proportional amount to what you invest in the fund.

Say a fund invests in 60 different stocks. For you to replicate this portfolio you'd have to research the 60 companies on your own, and decide how you want to structure the portfolio. This is a big task that could take a very long time if you want to do it properly.

Another huge perk of owning mutual fund shares, as opposed to owning shares in each company on your own, is that in order to acquire shares in those 60 different companies you'd have to place 60 different orders. These 60 separate transactions translate into a lot of commissions that you'd be paying to your broker. So between the time, labor, and commissions, it simply doesn't make sense for the average investor who wants diversification to try to do it on their own.

This isn't to say that mutual funds are the holy grail of investing. Mutual funds do have a management fee associated with them called the MER or Management Expense Ratio that is normally paid annually. Although it is not nearly as high as what some investment managers charge, it can still make a big impact over a period of time. You will also have to pay a sales charge sometimes referred to as a load. As the fund buys and sells shares they also have to pay commissions. Those commissions are deducted from the assets of the fund. The managers who run these funds are trying to beat the performance of an index by buying stocks they think will outperform the market. The commission costs are small relative to the size of the fund, but these costs do make a difference.

Something else to consider is the manager of the fund. Not all managers are created equal. Some outright suck. Others are decent. Then there is the odd one that is superb. The truth is that very very very few managers are actually able to beat the overall stock market consistently year after year, despite what you may think given their education and profession.

All in all, mutual funds are not without their flaws. They offer easy accessible diversification, but they often do not perform as well as we'd like them to and their fees can sometimes be pretty steep, as high as a couple percent per year. Remember that fees are the enemy of investors. Fees are what kill long run performance if they are not minimized. For these reasons, mutual funds are not the best investment vehicle for most investors. But if you still want to go this route make sure to do your homework, and find a fund with solid long-term performance and low fees. However, be aware that most funds are complete rip-offs. According to John

Bogle in The Little Book of Common Sense Investing, during the 35 year period from 1970 – 2005, out of the 355 equity mutual funds that were observed, only 3 have both survived and beat the S&P 500 by 2% or more. 3 out of 355 is less than 1%. Also, before you try to invest in these 3 remaining funds, think about the odds that they'll survive another 35 years. The odds are not weighted in their favor.

* * *

On the other hand, an index fund is simply a mutual fund that tracks the performance of an index such as the S&P 500. In all regards, an index fund is superior to a regular mutual fund. Remember how I said that most mutual fund managers suck because they rarely, if ever, beat the market? Say hello to the index fund. These don't employ fancy investment strategies. They're as basic as it gets. Basic is good! Overall an index fund will never beat the market, but it will match the market, and you as the investor, will earn a little less than the market return due to some small fees. However, history has shown that index funds will perform much better than your ordinary run of the mill mutual fund. Another perk of index funds, as opposed to regular mutual funds is that the MER is also going to be lower because they are much less management intensive.

Before we dive into Exchange Traded Funds (ETFs), let's talk about how we can really make index funds work for us in a way that will force us to save, and maximize our potential compounding (if done right). There is something that the investment community refers to as Dollar Cost Averaging. It enables investors to participate in the financial markets in a cost effective way without needing to invest a lot of money up front. But for some reason, you rarely hear about it in financial planning books. Okay so what is it? Dollar Cost Averaging is a system of buying stocks or mutual fund shares at regular intervals with a fixed dollar amount.

So how do you do it? Simple. You'll need to go to your bank and fill out a fund purchase application and set up a pre-authorized checking plan. Your bank will automatically debit your bank account for a specified amount each month. This amount will be invested in the fund. If you want to maximize the effects of compounding, instruct the fund management to reinvest the dividends you receive by purchasing more shares of the fund. At the end of each month you'll receive a statement outlining your holdings. Just sit back and watch your money grow!

Some of you may be wondering what

happens in the inevitable case where the market declines. Yes, your holdings will decrease in value, but a better way to look at it is if you are dollar cost averaging, you'll be getting more bang for your buck. When the markets move up and down, the index fund holdings will obviously go up and down with the market. By dollar cost averaging and buying during a down turn in the economy, you are effectively picking up more shares per fixed monthly investment than when the economy is roaring and shares are more expensive. In fact, many keen investors decide to invest more in pessimistic times to take advantage of the bargain pricing.

> *"Be fearful when others are greedy, be greedy when others are fearful"*
> - Warren Buffet

For those that are not mathematically inclined let's use a simple case where your fixed investment each month is $100. Let's use the simple example of a basic stock investment excluding transaction costs. Say you make a $100 investment into company XYZ each month. XYZ shares currently trade at $10. Fast-forward a couple months and the economy as a whole has taken a bit of a dip. Now XYZ shares are $5 each. If you're still investing $100 per month into XYZ, that means you're buying twice as many shares for the same amount of money as you were when the market was hot. Now fast-forward a year and the economy has picked back up again. Since you dollar cost averaged, you were able to pick up a bunch of shares at a cheap price relative to what they are now.

It is key to keep in mind that you aren't technically losing money when the market declines. Even though the value of your investments is decreasing, you only lose money when you sell for less than what you paid. Amateurs and other people who pay too close attention to the news and markets make the mistake of buying high and selling low. Buy and hold for a long period of time and tune out all the negative speculative garbage the news throws at you.

What a lot of people don't understand is that the value of nearly everything fluctuates. Buying real estate is just like investing in the stock market. The value of your home will fluctuate with the ups and downs in the real estate market, yet most people don't seem to think of that or pay much attention. People don't sell their house when they hear that housing prices are declining, but they sure are quick to dump shares whenever they get a whiff of negative market sentiment.

DCA Over a 20 Year Period

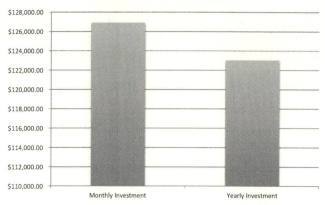

The above chart depicts what would happen if you saved $3,000 per year at 7% per year over 20 years. The left bar shows what would happen if you made monthly deposits of $250 ($250 x 12 = $3,000) and the right bar shows what would happen if you had invested $3000 in one lump sum each year. Why the difference? Compounding! Yes, yet another example of the magic of compound interest.

You earn more with the monthly deposits because you are earning interest sooner and for longer, than if you just deposit the total equivalent lump sum each year. The difference in this case is only about $4,000 over the course of 20 years but hey, 4 grand is 4 grand. If we extended this to a 40 year period the difference would be even greater.

Since we're on the topic I'll explain why dollar cost averaging doesn't work very well with individual stocks or anything that is traded on an exchange. Why? Commissions! Unless your investment amount each month is in the thousands it isn't feasible to be paying a commission each and every month. However, with index funds you can usually dollar cost average without paying fees every single month you invest.

ETFs

One of my favorite types of investment is the ETF. The easiest way to think of an exchange traded fund is like this: Tony goes out and buys a bunch of assets. These assets can be stocks, bonds, precious metals, commodities etc.. Then what Tony does is he sells "shares" of his fund of stocks, or whatever assets he has chosen to buy. As the assets in his fund appreciate, the value of the "shares", also increase and vice versa. The actual mechanics and creation of ETFs is slightly different but that topic is far beyond the scope of this book. So far it sounds like a mutual fund, right? Wrong! The perk of ETFs is that they are very simple to use and are traded on exchanges just like stocks. But the real upside to the ETF is the diversification and asset access it affords the holder at very low costs (usually). Instead of spending hours and hours picking stocks and racking up commissions, you can simply buy an ETF that will encompass a broad basket of stocks, commodities, bonds... or whatever you want in one package.

Again, just like a mutual fund. ETFs allow ordinary people to invest in oil, gold, palladium, expensive shares, or other assets that may not necessarily be available to them. Most importantly, you can purchase ETFs that are index tracking, similar to index funds discussed previously.

ETFs offer greater flexibility than mutual funds when it comes to trading. With mutual funds, purchases and sales take place directly between investors and the fund. The price of the funds' shares is not determined until the end of each business day when net asset value is determined. Net asset value is simply the total value of all the assets in the fund. An ETF, by comparison, is traded throughout the day like a stock and you can view real time trading prices. In order to invest in ETFs all you need to do is open a trading account. They don't cost anything to open. Just pay a visit to your local bank branch and they can set you up.

Due to the passive nature of indexed strategies, the internal expenses of most ETFs are considerably lower than those of many mutual funds. Those with the lowest expense ratios charge around 0.10% per year, while those with the highest expenses run about 1.25% per year. By comparison, the lowest mutual fund fees range from .01% to more than 10% per year for other funds. In my opinion, if you're paying more than 0.50% per year you're paying too much. Checkout Vanguard's ETFs. They have a vast array of products, and for the most part the MER on their ETFs are low. No, I'm not sponsored by them, but if anyone from Vanguard is reading this then hit me up! Below is an example of a great index tracking ETF with super low fees that also pays a dividend every 3 months.

Fund name Benchmark	Ticker	Fact sheet	Management fee*	MER	Distribution by unit
S&P 500 Index ETF	VFV	🗎	0.08%	0.08%	$0.18396
S&P 500 Index					

https://www.vanguardcanada.ca/advisors/etfs/etfs.htm

So to sum it up, ETFs are more liquid (more easily traded) than mutual funds, they can offer the same amount of diversification as a mutual fund, and they are generally cheaper to own than mutual funds. Just make sure to keep the fees as low as possible! The only catch is that, like trading stocks, when you buy or sell an ETF you have to pay a commission. However, commissions are pretty cheap, as you will learn later, and they aren't something you need to worry about as a passive long-term investor. ETFs and mutual funds are not generally meant to be bought and sold frequently. They are meant to be held for long periods of time so that you can reap the rewards of compounding. What's not to love?

Self-Directed Investing

I've been talking about investing and trading for a bit and some of you may be asking, "Okay so how do I actually do it?" Good question. It's pretty simple actually. I'd recommend going to your local bank branch and speaking with an advisor to see what they can offer you. Typically there are two ways you can go. The first is what they call "self directed" investing where you place your own trades and manage your portfolio all by yourself. The second is when you're set up with an investment manager who will give you advice and ultimately take care of your investments for you (for a price). We already know how the investment managers perform...

Many people choose to go the investment manager route due to their lack of understanding of investing. I have no exposure to dealing with investment managers, since I chose the self-directed route from the beginning. However, if you do choose to go with a manager, ensure that you UNDERSTAND what they're proposing, and if you don't then ask as many questions as you need until you understand it. Don't feel bad about asking questions, it's your money on the line after all! If they can't explain it to you then find someone competent to do so. Don't just go with whatever it is that they're proposing because complexity usually isn't a good thing. A study conducted by The New York Times found that between the years of 1993 – 2007, funds chosen by financial advisors earned 40% less than a broad market index fund.[3]

Do some homework. It's key to go in with knowledge of various investment products so you don't end up mindlessly following the advice of an advisor and making sub-optimal investment decisions. You control what you do with your money, not them, so don't let the fancy finance lingo blind your judgment. As a general rule for pretty much anything, don't do it unless you understand it.

If you decide to take the self-directed option, go to your bank and tell them that you'd like a self-directed investing account. They will ask for some information and set you up with an account that will be active and ready for use within a couple business days.

In addition to self-directed investing via your bank, you could opt for an online brokerage that will allow you to perform similar functions as you could with a bank brokerage account. In my experience some have been a pain to set up accounts with, and therefore I prefer to go through my bank to keep things simple and centralized. Plus, I don't actively manage my investments, so I have no need for the bells and whistles that some platforms offer. However, most online brokerages offer very competitive fees so they are worth considering.

Online brokerages do have their perks. Lots of them nowadays have fairly well developed online platforms with intuitive user interfaces and good functionality. In addition, many of them have cheap commissions on trades usually in the $4 – $8 range per trade. To remain competitive the banks have responded by lowering their commission charges to a similar range.

Bank Accounts and GICs

I'm going to assume that anyone reading this has at least a savings account. Your bank pays you next to nothing in interest on the money you have in your account. The problem with this is that after you factor in inflation, you're literally making nothing at all. The upside to having a savings account is that your money is guaranteed to be secure by the Canadian Deposit Insurance Guarantee up to $100,000. Also, most of the big banks offer very low to zero fees for youth and students. Or if you're in the United States, your bank deposits are insured up to $250,000 by the Federal Deposit Insurance Corporation.

Something else that is worth pointing out is that once bank customers are no longer eligible for youth or student accounts, the only chequing accounts available will incur monthly service fees, and possibly other fees as well. The only way around the monthly service fee is generally to maintain a high monthly minimum balance. Actual savings accounts may not charge a monthly fee, but the charge for individual debits will be very high. It's a RUDE awakening for those who aren't used to the fees.

Some banks also offer what are called tiered savings accounts. These are accounts where the bank will pay you additional interest if your account balance remains above a certain amount (usually a minimum of a few thousand dollars). The reason they are called tiered savings accounts is because as you meet certain savings thresholds, the interest you receive increases. Transaction fees for these types of accounts can be higher. Keep that in mind. These are usually good options if you're fairly certain that your account balance won't dip below whatever the threshold amount is.

Let's say you have $1000 lying around that you know you won't need to use for a year or two. Instead of putting that money into a savings account, you could opt for a GIC or Term Deposit (They're essentially the same). GIC stands for Guaranteed Investment Certificate. How these work is you lend money to a financial institution for a few months or years, and they pay you a rate of interest for having lent them your money. The only catch is that you can't touch that money until the specified lending period is up unless you want to pay a fee. Generally, the longer the term of the GIC, the higher the interest rate you receive. However, the interest rates at the time of the writing of this book are insultingly low. You're not even beating inflation.

When your GIC matures the institution will return your money plus interest. They may also give you the option to roll-over the matured GIC into a new one. GICs and Term Deposits are most useful when interest rates are high.

There are also Market Linked GICs. These are tied to the performance of the stock market. The upside is that you can earn a higher rate of interest if the stock market performs well. Also, like regular GICs, your principal is guaranteed. The downside is that the amount of interest you can earn is capped at a certain rate, and if the stock market does not perform well, you may receive no interest at all. In fact, the interest you may receive is taxed as interest income instead of capital gains, which means that it's taxed at a higher rate.

Sure GICs are comfortable and stable, but the markets don't reward comfort and stability. If you want to make money you're going to have to deal with some level of risk. GICs have a place in the financial product spectrum, but in my opinion they aren't worth it. Tying up my money for a period of time only to earn an embarrassingly low rate of interest doesn't appeal to me.

Since we're on the topic of bank accounts and GICs, I'll finish this section with a basic explanation of the business model of a bank – yes, banks are businesses. It's really straightforward. At their core, all they do is borrow your money (your deposits) and pay you for lending them your money (the interest you earn). Then they lend the money to others at higher rates of interest (think mortgages and car loans) and pocket the difference between the interest rate they pay you and the interest they charge to borrowers. The difference is called the Net Interest Income. In addition to net interest income, the banks make a lot of money from the fees that they charge their clients – ATM fees, overdraft charges, foreign currency transactions, late payment fees etc. It should go without saying that you should avoid these fees. Banks are in the business of making money.

RRSPs & TFSAs

RRSPs

I'm sure you've heard your parents talk about RRSPs before (the American equivalent is the 401(k)). What exactly is an RRSP? RRSP stands for Registered Retirement Savings Plan, which is meant to help Canadians save and invest for retirement. Essentially, anyone who has income is eligible to set up an RRSP. Yes, anyone. You don't have to be 18. As long as you have claimed income via an annual tax return you're eligible. You can set up an RRSP at a number of financial institutions such as banks, credit unions, mutual funds, insurance companies etc.. And you're allowed to have as many RRSPs as you see fit, although it's probably wise to keep things fairly simple and centralized.

An RRSP allows you to invest in pretty much whatever you want from stocks, to bonds, to GICs... Recall the lesson on compounding and how investing earlier is better than later? Well, investing in RRSPs is no different. You'd be much better off saving for retirement when you're 20 as opposed to 40, since by waiting you will lose out on 20 years of compounding. Those 20 years will make a huge difference. You've probably had enough with the charts and graphs by now, but it is crucial to understand the power of compounding. Let's say you start investing $5,000 each year at 6% and retire when you're 60. Illustrated below is what you'd have at age 60 if you started investing at ages 20, 30, 40.

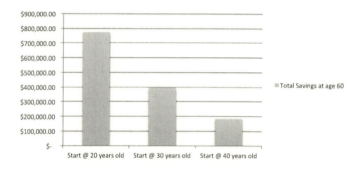

Okay, so back to RRSPs. The major benefit of an RRSP is that it allows for an immediate tax deduction for the money you've invested. If you make $80,000 per year, and you contribute $10,000 of that to your RRSP, and if your marginal tax rate is 40%, you will get $4,000 in tax savings for that year. This means you'll pay $28,000 instead of $32,000 in taxes that year.

Regular Tax Payment: $80,000 X .40 = $32,000
Tax Savings from RRSP Contributions: $10,000 X .40
= $4,000
Amount of Tax Paid: $32,000 - $4,000 = $28,000

You are, however, limited to the amount you can contribute to your RRSP in any one year. The limit depends on your income. The limit is 18% of the tax years' earned income up to a maximum amount of around $25,000 (the max contribution amount is changed frequently). A second benefit of an RRSP is if you did not max out in previous years, you have what is called a carry-forward, meaning that your limit can be greater. In other words, if you don't make an RRSP contribution this year, or you contribute less than your maximum limit, the unused amount is carried forward and can be used in any future year.

In addition to stocks, bonds, mutual funds, and GICs, you can "buy" RRSPs that focus on certain types of investments. Guaranteed Plans ensure you won't lose your capital, and will earn a low rate of interest, so that you know exactly how much money you will have at a future date. Variable Rate Plans don't necessarily guarantee the safety of your capital, but they are often very safe and have the potential to provide superior returns as compared to Guaranteed Plans.

Typically, novice investors allow the financial institution that set up their RRSP to put their money in eligible RRSP investments. However, you can opt for a self directed RRSP that allows you to choose the investments you want. If you set up a self directed RRSP, you can transfer money into it that has previously been put into other RRSPs to create a single consolidated RRSP. This is the best route to go, in my opinion, as long as you know what you're doing.

Another point to note about RRSPs is that you can withdraw money from them at anytime before retirement without a fee. BUT, you will have to pay taxes on the money you take out unless you're participating in a Home Buyers Plan (HBP) or a Life Long Learning Plan (LLP) and you'll permanently lose the contribution room you originally used to make the contribution.

A Home Buyers Plan allows first time homebuyers to borrow up to $25,000 from their RRSP to aid in financing the purchase of a home. This money has to be repaid within 15 years. A Lifelong Learning Plan is for people that want to go back to school and want to borrow money to fund their tuition. With the LLP you can borrow $10,000 per year up to a maximum of $20,000 over four years. This loan must be paid back within 10 years. RRSPs mature when you turn 71, and at that point you have three options.

First, you could convert it into a lump-sum payout. Since you must withdraw all funds from your RRSP by the end of the calendar year in which your 71st birthday is, this option is basically forced upon you unless you make other arrangements. The money that is withdrawn is subject to taxes.

Second, you can convert your RRSP into an annuity. As previously discussed, an annuity is a steady stream of cash paid at set intervals for a finite period of time. These are great for people that want the peace of mind of knowing they will have a stream of income for the rest of their lives.

Third, you can convert your RRSP into a Registered Retirement Income Fund. A RRIF will extend the tax benefits of an RRSP by allowing you to withdraw money over time instead of all at once, thus potentially avoiding the high tax associated with a single lump sum payment. With a RRIF you are required to withdraw a minimum amount every year. You're probably asking yourself "Why would I do this when I can just opt for an annuity?" The real benefit of a RRIF is that it allows you to preserve your investments so that they can continue to grow. Also, annuities offered to you via your bank or financial institution have fees. Fees are bad. Minimize fees as much as possible!

TFSAs

A Tax Free Savings Account sounds fairly self-explanatory, however, it is far from your plain vanilla savings account. A TFSA is actually a very powerful tool that anybody over the age of 18 can use to build wealth. Unlike an RRSP, contributions to a TFSA are not deductible for income tax purposes. The best part about TFSAs is that any amount contributed, as well as any income generated in the account, is tax-free even when it's withdrawn. It's essentially a mirror image of the RRSP since you contribute after tax dollars and your withdrawals are tax-free. The United States has something very similar to the TFSA, it's called the Roth IRA.

In a TFSA you can hold stocks, bonds, mutual funds, ETFs, GICs, and cash just like with an RRSP. These investments will grow tax-free. That means that you won't have to pay tax on dividends, capital gains, or the interest earned by your investments in your TFSA. This is a big deal!

You can only contribute up to the TFSA

contribution limit. Unused TFSA contribution room can be carried forward to later years. The total amount of TFSA withdrawals in a calendar year is added to the TFSA contribution room for the next calendar year. You are also entitled to the lifetime contribution room of your TFSA each year after your 18th birthday, which means that if your 18th birthday is today, but you don't start your TFSA until you're say 28 years old, you'll have $55,000 ($5500 x 10) of contribution room as of the calendar year in which you turn 28. Although you don't get the tax deductions on contributions as in an RRSP, you can withdraw funds from your .TFSA whenever you please, and then replace them the following year. However, this also can be a problem if you like to spend money. Don't withdraw unless it's absolutely necessary.

As of the writing of this short book you are allowed to contribute up to $5,500 a year to your TFSA, however these contribution numbers often change. The downside is that if you over-contribute you'll have to pay some fees for doing so.

Another benefit of the TFSA is that you can keep contributing to it as long as you please. So if you're 77 years old you still have the ability to grow your money tax free in your TFSA.

* * *

TFSAs and RRSPs both have their perks, and ideally you want to max out both every single year. This isn't realistic for most people as many are not high-income earners. Everyone has a different financial situation, so the key here is to make the right choice and prioritize when choosing between contributing to a TFSA or an RRSP. Having said that, saving is saving. Whether you choose the TFSA or the RRSP or both, you're not screwing up because ultimately you're making the right choice to save rather than to spend. We're humans, not computers, and we can't and often don't make "optimal" decisions. Saving for retirement is a step in the right direction regardless which way you choose. Let's now look at when it makes sense to use the RRSP and the TFSA.

It makes the most sense to contribute to your RRSP when you're in a higher tax bracket, to maximize the tax deductions, and withdraw when you're in a low tax bracket, since withdrawals from your RRSP are taxable. Withdrawing when you're in the high tax bracket basically negates the benefit of having an RRSP, since you'd be taxed at a higher rate that would offset the tax deductions when you contributed. So the bottom line is withdraw when your tax rate is lower than your tax rate was when you made contributions. Typically this is the case for most people. Rarely will a person's retirement income be greater than their income during their prime working years. Thus they would be in different tax brackets in the different stages of life.

For you to get the most out of a TFSA it makes the most sense to contribute when you're in a low tax bracket, and withdraw when you're in a high tax bracket since withdrawals are not taxable and the investments in your TFSA grow tax free.

For those that have lower income, usually when you're younger, a TFSA can work a lot better than an RRSP, because your income will likely increase as you get older, and thus you will move up in the tax brackets. In this time, if you only focus on contributing to your TFSA, you will be building up contribution room in your RRSP, so that when you make it to the higher tax brackets you'll be able to take advantage of the tax benefits available.

Finally, for those that have high income, try to maximize both the RRSP and TFSA. A strategy that many financial planners suggest is to use the RRSP tax refund to fund your TFSA. Reinvesting your tax refund is the best way to make the most of your RRSP. We have already looked at the potential growth of maximizing your TFSA and RRSP. That should be motivation enough to make contributions, even if it's only a small amount each month.

Retirement Saving Goals

Alright, so in a perfect world you would max out your RRSP and TFSA contributions each and every year. Yearly maximum contribution amounts change frequently so the figures in the charts below are based on the 2018 numbers. The 2018 RRSP maximum amount is $26,230 and the TFSA maximum is $5,500. That means if your income is high enough you can contribute a maximum of $31,730 per year. If you were to contribute this amount over the course of 40 years earning a moderate rate of return of 6%, you would accumulate nearly $4.8M!!! Not a bad amount to retire on considering some experts say that you need around $500,000 to retire.

Don't forget that RRSP withdrawals are taxable at your marginal tax rate. The potential actual cash you will have to retire on is going to be less than what is shown below. If you withdraw all of your RRSP in one lump sum, you will likely pay tax at a higher rate than if you were to convert the RRSP money into an annuity or RRIF and receive steady payments. Another thing to think about is the tax benefits of having an RRSP. You get a tax refund on your contributions which is what makes the RRSP such an effective tool. Obviously the best course of action is to reinvest these tax refunds, but most people don't do that.

Effectively what the RRSP curve in the graph on the following page represents is saving $26,230 per year earning 6% per year. The reinvestment of tax refunds and the tax upon withdrawal of your RRSP has not been accounted for due to the numerous ways a person can go about managing his/her money.

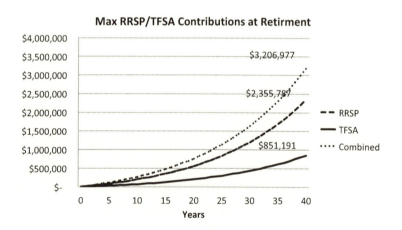

For many, it is rather idealistic to assume that you can contribute north of $30,000 to retirement each and every year. $30,000 is a lot of money, and only a small proportion of the population will be able to save this much and have high enough income to do so. But if you can, do it! More is better, but not at the expense of enjoying some of the luxuries of life.

Below is another chart that illustrates fractions of the maximum contribution amounts contributed each year earning 6%, again not factoring the tax you'd pay on your RRSP withdrawals. We can say these figures in the charts are inflation adjusted, if we assume we are going to be earning a market rate of return of 8%, since policy makers try to keep inflation somewhere in the neighborhood of 2% per year. What you can take away from this is that in order to meet the experts' $500,000 magic number, you need to save 1/8 of the maximum contribution amount each year. This works out to $3,858.75. We'll look further into this later.

Remember those annuity formulas we covered at the beginning of the book? You can use those to calculate the potential future value of your retirement savings, assuming you contribute the same amount each year. Essentially, all I did to calculate these numbers and generate these charts was use the FV annuity formula in Excel. Again, something that will take you 30 seconds to learn on YouTube if you are inclined to do so.

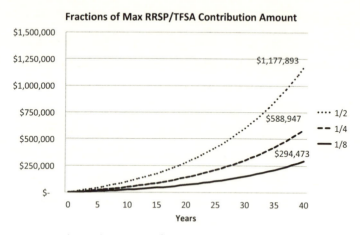

Fractions of Max RRSP/TFSA Contribution Amount

I don't buy that $500,000 retirement number mentioned previously because everyone has a different situation. So how much money do you need in order to retire comfortably? It's a tough question to answer because for each person or couple, different needs and lifestyles must be addressed on a case-by-case basis. There is no one-size-fits-all amount. Lifestyle, past income, and retirement age are big factors. During your working years you likely may have allocated a lot of money towards a mortgage, raising kids, clothing for work, retirement saving, income tax etc. Hopefully you won't have many of these costs when you're retired. Because of this, you won't need as much income to support yourself. On the other hand, like most retirees, you may want to do a lot of traveling, or other things you didn't get a chance to do earlier in life. Regardless, you're likely not going to require as much money to live comfortably.

A big consideration to take into account is the rising average lifespan of the population. As time goes on, the average human lifespan is only going to increase, which means the longer you live the more money you'll need to sustain yourself. Technology is advancing incredibly quickly. I'm 24 at the time of writing this, and I'm confident that the average age of the population will be close to 100 years by the time I'm 70. This means that in order for me to retire at 65 I'll need a lot more money to sustain myself throughout the remainder of my life. You're going to need to make your retirement savings go further. Don't plan to out-live your savings! It's always good to have too much rather than too little. The reality of it is that you're going to have to be a millionaire to retire.

Experts and studies say that you need around 60% of your working income to retire on.[2] So if you, or your spouse and yourself combined, were making $100,000 per year during your working years, then you should be able to live comfortably on approximately $60,000 without compromising the lifestyle you've become accustomed to. It's worth noting that if you're married your cost per person to live is less than if you are single because two people double up on many everyday living expenses, so overall on a per person basis they require less.

You also have to think about how long you think you'll live. A grim topic, I know. But this is simply part of the process. Let's say you retire at 65 and believe you'll live to be 90. This means that you'll need at least 25 years' worth of savings to get you to 90. 25 x $60,000 = $1.5M. This is crude math because there is no way to exactly determine the amount you'll need, but you're better off over saving than under-saving. According to the Survey of Household Spending 2009, the average senior couple spends $54,100 per year, while median spending for senior couples is only $39,400 per year. Once you have a rough sense of what retirement will cost, the next thing you could do is figure out the portion covered by government benefits. Yes, you could get government benefits when you retire! Looks like they aren't stealing all of our money after all! But we aren't even going to look into government benefits because 1. Who knows if they will even exist by the time you're old enough to use them and 2. You shouldn't rely on the government to help you out in retirement.

Alright, so let's revisit roughly how much saving you actually need to retire. Earlier it was mentioned that roughly 60% of your yearly working income should do it. Let's say if we have $80,000 in pre-retirement income, and we apply the 60% rule, we get $48,000. Multiply $48,000 by 25, assuming we retire at 65 and plan to live to 90, we find that we must save $1,200,000.

$1,200,000 is a lot of money, and by no means am I saying that this is some golden number that you have to hit. However, through the power of compounding, it is a realistic goal for most people. If you are disciplined and make good use of your TFSA and RRSP, along side other savings, you can accumulate it. The median Canadian family income in 2013 was $76,000, therefore, to accumulate $1,200,000 shouldn't be a huge challenge especially since you will likely have other savings and investments in addition to your RRSP and TFSA.[17]

I'm sure a lot of people would disagree with me saying that $1,200,000 is achievable. Well, a lot of people also don't know very much about finance and how money works, and they also don't start saving early in life. However, there are some people that have jobs that just don't pay enough for them to be able to retire on a high six-figure number.

Remember, this isn't a competition, this is about you and your spouse (if you have one) being happy and comfortable when you're older. There are many couples that get by each year on $60,000 during their working years and are totally content. There's nothing wrong with that as long as you can adequately provide for you and your family. However, bringing in $60,000 per year is not an admirable goal. Aim higher.

A retirement survey by HSBC found that 48% of pre-retiree Canadians have not started or are not currently saving for retirement. Please do not become one of the 48%. SAVE FOR RETIREMENT EARLY! Even if you can't afford to contribute a whole lot of money, anything is better than nothing – but figure out how to save more.

Saving and Budgeting Basics

Well you've made it this far, I'd say you should give yourself a pat on the back. So far we've talked about the time value of money, interest rates, credit, mortgages, mutual funds, TFSAs, ETFS, diversification and retirement planning... To conclude this short book we're going to discuss saving money and budgeting. Learning how to budget and manage your money is crucial to building wealth and living a sustainable life. This is the most important chapter in the entire book. If you don't master how to manage your income and expenses then you're screwed. Period.

Saving seems to be extremely hard for most. You often hear statistics that people are spending far more than they're saving, and that they're not even close to being prepared for retirement. Many people get their pay cheques, and are quick to spend everything on any shiny object that catches their eye.

Everyone wants you to spend more money, from your friends, to your real estate agent, to the dishonest mechanic trying to convince you that your car needs additional repairs.

People that live within their means, and consequently spend less than they earn, live happier lives because they don't have to worry about their financial future. Don't let yourself become consumed with consumption.[7] People that live within their means are not caught up in the "status battle" to see who has a bigger RV, or nicer clothing, or the biggest house. Being in a never-ending competition with everyone else is foolish and emotionally and financially taxing. It's not your perceived wealth that matters, it's your actual wealth. Don't confuse the cost of living with the standard of living.

Before we go further, it should be mentioned that spending is okay. You don't need to be ultra frugal and save every nickel and dime. Take vacations and buy nice things, just don't compromise your future by doing so. There's no point saving absolutely everything and living like a bum if you have millions in the bank. Go ahead and treat yourself if you honestly can afford to do so.

Want to know the best way to save money? When you get paid, first save 10% (or more), then spend the rest on your needs and wants, in that order! This way you don't even have to worry about saving. Just save the money, get it out of the way first, then move on with your life. Simple as that. Give it a shot! It's a lot easier to manage your money when the saving is already taken care of right off the bat. Many online banking platforms even let you set up automatic withdrawals and deposits so that you can automatically withdraw money from one account and deposit it into another, such as a TFSA.

"Do not save what is left after spending, but spend what is left after saving"
- Warren Buffett

Everyone has their own unique situation. Everyone has different expenses and lifestyles. Therefore, what I am about to explain is by no means set in stone. Everyone's situation will affect how they allocate their money. The following is merely a framework for you to get a basic understanding of how one can responsibly use their money.

There are 5 main categories to which someone may allocate his/her money. These are housing, transportation, savings/investing, debt, and everything else (other).

Housing refers to anything home related such

as mortgage payments, rent, utilities, maintenance, and any other costs that go into putting a roof over your head.

Transportation is fairly self-explanatory, but I'll go through it anyway. These costs may include car payments, maintenance, gas, insurance, bus passes, scooters... you get the idea. Whatever it costs you to get from A to B. However, I'd argue that a new set of wheels, or an exhaust system, shouldn't fall into this section, since these are discretionary items and are not totally necessary for your day-to-day transportation. All of you car people out there might not want to admit to this but it's true (at least for budgeting purposes).

Savings/Investing means anything from your basic savings account to RRSPs to self-directed investing. This is the one category that you want to maximize. It never hurts to save more if you're able to. This section does not refer to saving for stuff that you want like a new computer, those gorgeous heels you saw at the mall, or a new snowboard. These planned expenditures fall into the Other category, as will be discussed later.

Debt. Credit card debt, lines of credit, loans of any sort... All of these things and anything related to you spending money before you have it, or borrowing money, falls into the debt category. Best to keep this one small. It also should go without saying that paying down any debt you may have, as fast as possible, should be a priority of yours, even if that means reducing the money you allocate to planned expenditures or discretionary purchases. Yeah, it might be tough to hold up on that new Xbox or purse, but trust me, in the long run you'll be much better off and much happier. Also, the quicker you pay off debt, the more time and money you have available to save and invest!

Other is whatever else that doesn't fall into one of the previous four categories. Planned expenditures, clothes, food, phone bills, vacations, drinks... and whatever else you can think of will be in this category.

On the following page is what I believe to be a solid budget framework for anyone of any age that has to deal with all 5 of the "expense" categories previously listed. These are just guides. If you can only afford to save 5% then do it, because that's still better than nothing, but also think about how you're allocating your income so you can maximize your savings.

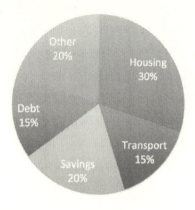

Everyone has a different situation in terms of how they need to allocate their money, so the pie chart on the following page could illustrate how a student living at home may decide to allocate his/her money. Notice that there is no Housing category because we're assuming here that you're not paying rent. For this reason, you may have more disposable income, for planned spending or other things, which is why the Other category increased to 30%. Yes, saving 40% is an ambitious number but if you're young and living at home it's not unrealistic. Just remember the power of compounding, and how investing more when you're young means you'll have even more when you're older.

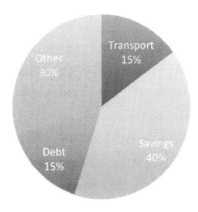

Now let's examine a case where you not only don't have housing expenses to worry about, but are also fortunate enough to not have transportation expenses either. These numbers are by no means set in stone, but they should provide you with a good framework and way of thinking about how you allocate your money.

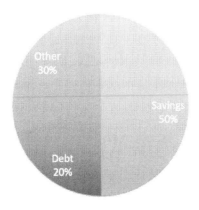

It's pretty idealistic to assume that a person can save 50% or more of their income, but it's possible and a small fraction of the population actually do this. Likely, if you don't have to worry about a car or mortgage, your Debt and Other categories won't be too much different from the first scenario I presented which took into account all 5 areas of money allocation. This is usually the case for a lot of university and high school students.

If, however, you're a student with a bunch of student loans to pay off then surely you should make that a priority over saving 50% of your money. Your debt category might be upwards of 50%, but that's okay as long as the money is going towards paying down your student loans and not taking trips to Cancun.

In my opinion, the easiest way to keep track of your expenses and manage your finances is to use Microsoft Excel. If you have a Mac you might want to check out the app called Numbers. It gives you a bunch of Excel templates that you can use for budgeting and various other things. Also, there are expense tracking apps out there, but likely they don't do anything that you can't do yourself in Excel. You don't need to be a finance guru to know how to use Excel or Numbers. They're pretty easy, and I'm sure there are plenty of YouTube videos to teach you how to use them. Alternatively, you could go old school and use a pen and a notebook. Whatever floats your boat.

Go through your bills, receipts, credit card statements etc. and make a list of your expenses, make a budget, record the actual expense incurred, calculate the difference, make a couple of notes, and look at the areas where you are over spending and consider correcting your spending habits. Simple as that.

On the following page are a couple examples of how you might want to go about constructing your budget. Both of these are very easy to make in Excel. As previously mentioned, look up a YouTube video, and within minutes you'll have your own budget spreadsheet that you can edit. For this whole budgeting thing to work you NEED to stay on the ball and record everything. This stuff isn't very difficult, you just need to stay disciplined. After each week keep track of the money you've spent by recording the expenses in your spreadsheet. It will take you no more than 15 minutes to do this. At the end of each week I make sure to spend a few minutes updating and reviewing my budget so I can be sure I'm on track.

	Expenses	Budgeted	Actual	Difference	Comments
	Rent	$ 1,200.00	$ 1,200.00	$ -	
Housing	Utilities	$ 200.00	$ 150.00	$ 50.00	
	Tenant Insurance	$ 20.00	$ 20.00	$ -	
	Car Payment	$ 400.00	$ 400.00	$ -	
Transport	Car Insurance	$ 150.00	$ 150.00	$ -	
	Gas	$ 150.00	$ 160.00	-$ 10.00	
Savings	Savings	$ 1,250.00	$ 1,200.00	$ 50.00	
Debt	Credit Card	$ 400.00	$ 375.00	$ 25.00	
	Line of Credit	$ 400.00	$ 405.00	-$ 5.00	
	Clothes	$ 100.00	$ 50.00	$ 50.00	
	Food	$ 400.00	$ 420.00	-$ 20.00	
Other	Phone/Internet	$ 100.00	$ 100.00	$ -	
	Night Out	$ 100.00	$ 90.00	$ 10.00	
	Miscellaneous	$ 100.00	$ 115.00	-$ 15.00	
	Total	$ 4,970.00	$ 4,835.00	$ 135.00	

My Budget

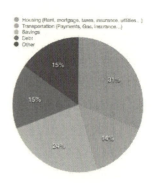

INCOME	
Paycheck	$4,000
Side Business	$1,200
TOTAL INCOME	$5,200

EXPENSES	
Housing (Rent, mortgage, taxes, insurance, utilities...)	$1,600
Transportation (Payments, Gas, Insurance ...)	$750
Savings	$1,250
Debt	$800
Other	$800
TOTAL EXPENSES	$5,200

Something I find that works well alongside budget building is cost forecasting. By this I mean forecasting your expenses in advance so you have a better idea of what you will be spending your money on and when. Not every month will look the same in terms of your expenses. If there are any larger planned expenditures in the foreseeable future such as vacations, gift giving seasons, new car etc... it helps for you record all of these so that it's easier for you to plan ahead instead of being squeezed at last minute to fund whatever you need to pay for. This is sort of like in school when your teachers always tell you to study throughout the year instead of cramming last minute. Proper planning goes a long way.

Another instance where cost forecasting really helps is if you're a student with a summer job, or a part time job you work during the year and a full time job during the summer etc. When you're working and making money it's easy to start spending erratically on things you don't need because having steady cash-flow is not something you're used to. After all, it's human nature to spend all of our disposable income and rationalize those expenses as needs.[6]

Expense forecasting will allow you to more accurately predict your cash-flows in and out, so you can be prepared ahead of time. Also, being aware and visually seeing large infrequent expenses on your cost forecast will enable you to make better financial decisions. Those big expenses will be in the back of your mind, and you will say to yourself, "Maybe I shouldn't impulsively buy those $500 shoes because Christmas is in 3 months and I should be saving my money." Also try to ask yourself before you make some large impulsive discretionary purchase, "Do I really need this? Will I be as pumped a year from now about this thing as I am now?" Impulsive purchases are similar to a kid who gets a Happy Meal toy – there's a lot of initial excitement, then after a short period they lose interest.

To some people, expense forecasting will seem like pure common sense. Quite frankly it is. It's just that most people don't do it. On the following page is the template I use for myself.

EXPENSES

	January	February	March	April	May	June	July	August	September	October	November	December	Total Expenses
Gas	$ 150	$ 150	$ 150	$ 150	$ 150	$ 150	$ 150	$ 150	$ 150	$ 150	$ 150	$ 150	
Car Insurance	$ 200	$ 200	$ 200	$ 200	$ 200	$ 200	$ 200	$ 200	$ 200	$ 200	$ 200	$ 200	
Food	$ 650	$ 650	$ 650	$ 650	$ 650	$ 650	$ 650	$ 650	$ 650	$ 650	$ 650	$ 650	
Clothing	$ 200	$ -	$ -	$ 200	$ -	$ -	$ 200	$ -	$ -	$ 200	$ -	$ -	
Holidays/Special Occasions	$ 150	$ 400	$ -	$ 480	$ -	$ -	$ 1,250	$ -	$ -	$ 200	$ 300	$ 300	
Miscellaneous	$ 250	$ 250	$ 250	$ 250	$ 500	$ 1,800	$ 400	$ 180	$ 200	$ 200	$ 200	$ 200	
Phone	$ 85	$ 85	$ 85	$ 85	$ 85	$ 85	$ 85	$ 85	$ 85	$ 85	$ 85	$ 85	
Rent	$ 1,000	$ 1,000	$ 1,000	$ 1,000	$ 1,000	$ 1,000	$ 1,000	$ 1,000	$ 1,000	$ 1,000	$ 1,000	$ 1,000	
Total	$ 2,685	$ 2,735	$ 2,335	$ 3,015	$ 2,585	$ 3,885	$ 3,935	$ 2,265	$ 2,285	$ 2,685	$ 2,585	$ 2,585	$ 33,580

INCOME

	January	February	March	April	May	June	July	August	September	October	November	December	Total Income
Pay Cheque	$ 4,625	$ 4,625	$ 4,625	$ 4,625	$ 4,625	$ 4,625	$ 4,625	$ 4,625	$ 4,625	$ 4,625	$ 4,625	$ 4,625	
Other	$ 400	$ 400	$ 400	$ 400	$ 400	$ 400	$ 400	$ 400	$ 400	$ 400	$ 400	$ 400	
Total	$ 5,025	$ 5,025	$ 5,025	$ 5,025	$ 5,025	$ 5,025	$ 5,025	$ 4,625	$ 4,625	$ 4,625	$ 4,625	$ 4,625	$ 58,300
Net	$ 2,340	$ 2,290	$ 2,690	$ 2,010	$ 2,440	$ 1,140	$ 1,090	$ 2,360	$ 2,340	$ 1,940	$ 2,040	$ 2,040	

Savings $ 24,720

SALARY

Yearly Salary	$ 75,000
Tax Rate	26%
Post Tax Salary	$ 55,500

SAVINGS GOALS

Yearly Savings Goal %	25%
Yearly Savings Goal Amount	$ 18,750
Savings Goal Per Month	$ 1,563
Actual FCF (Net Income)	$ 24,720
Actual FCF / Month	$ 2,060

SAVINGS/INVESTMENTS

18-01-01		Deposit		EoY	
Chequing + Savings	$ 38,500	$ 3,708		$ 42,208	
TFSA	$ 905	$ 5,500		$ 6,405	
Other	$ -	$ 15,512		$ 15,512	
Total	$ 39,405	$ 24,720		$ 64,125	

Savings Growth

Okay, by now you've probably really had it with all the charts and graphs, but I feel that they help drive home the points I am trying to make. I just really want to emphasize the benefit of planning, starting early, and being disciplined.

The chart below shows how much money you'd have by age 65 if you were to start saving $1200 per year ($100 per month), at ages 25, 35, and 45 respectively, and you invested the $1200 at the end of each year and earned 7%. There is no better way to illustrate the power of compounding than seeing something like this.

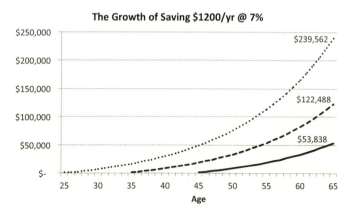

If you were to start investing $1200 per year at age 25, after 40 years of compounding and saving, by 65 years old you would have roughly

$240,000. Now what happens if you wait 10 years to start saving? If you started saving $1200 per year at age 35, you'd have around $122,000 by the time you're 65. And if you started at 45, you'd have about $54,000. So if you wait 10 years you end up with half of what you would have had if you started at 25. You're reducing your savings period by 25% yet you're losing out on 50% of what you could have had when you retire. If you wait 20 years then you will end up having one fifth of what you would have had if you started 20 years sooner. You're reducing your savings years by 50% and you're only left with 20% of what you could have had at age 65. The fractions just get smaller and smaller the longer you wait. START ASAP!

The key lesson here is to spend less than you earn and know that saving money alone will never make you rich. Don't save for the sake of saving. Save to invest and grow your money. Money sitting in a bank account is dead money. Make it work for you.

Final Comments

I know that finance and money talk may not be the most captivating and interesting topic. In fact, it can get pretty dry. However, there are just some things that you need to know as an adult. I'm hoping that you got to the end of this book and now feel like you have some of the foundational knowledge of personal finance under your belt. Like I said at the beginning of the book, you won't be able to memorize all of this information at once. Revisit topics you need clarification on, and read other more detailed books to get a deeper understanding. The idea was to introduce you to things you may not have been aware of before.

My hope is that now you feel more confident and more inclined to read more and learn more. It might not seem like a big deal now, but I guarantee that when you're 50 you're going to thank yourself for learning more about this stuff as a young person. The more you learn the more you earn.

Here are a few tips to guarantee a bright financial future:

- Spend less than you earn.
- Avoid instant gratification by delaying consumption.
- Pay off high-interest debt ASAP.
- Never buy or lease a new car.
- Never over extend yourself for the purchase of a home.
- Always pay off your credit card on time.
- Don't save for the sake of saving. Save to invest.
- Start investing early!

Connect with me on social media and let me know what you think of the book!

Instagram: @antoni.zr

Linkedin: Tony Randhawa

Recommended Books

I love reading. It's something I make time for everyday. Below are some interesting books on various topics ranging from personal finance to entrepreneurship. All of the books listed contain great information and I would recommend them to anyone. Invest in yourself! Learn as much as you can while you're young.

Personal Finance

Unshakeable
The Wealthy Barber
The Wealthy Barber Returns

Investing:

Beat The Crowd
Charlie Munger The Complete Investor
The Little Book of Common Sense Investing

Canadian Real Estate

Making Money in Real Estate
Cash Flow for Life

Random Interesting Books

Freakonomics
Superfreakonomics
Think Like a Freak
Abundance
The Subtle Art of Not Giving a F*ck

Bibliography

1. Annual Percentage Rate (APR) Definition | Investopedia. (2003). Retrieved July 08, 2016, from http://www.investopedia.com/terms/a/apr.asp

2. Aston, D. (2012, May 08). How much do you need to retire well? - Canadian Business - Your Source For Business News. Retrieved July 08, 2016, from http://www.canadianbusiness.com/investing/how-much-do-you-need-to-retire-well/

3. Bogle, J. C. (2007). The little book of common sense investing: The only way to guarantee your fair share of stock market returns. Hoboken, NJ: John Wiley & Sons.

4. Calculating The Present And Future Value Of Annuities | Investopedia. (2003). Retrieved July 08, 2016, from http://www.investopedia.com/articles/03/101503.asp

5. Canada Pension Plan vs. Old Age Security - the differences explained - Business: Tax Season - CBC News. (2013, January 07). Retrieved July 08, 2016, from http://www.cbc.ca/news/business/taxes/canada-pension-plan-vs-old-age-security-the-differences-explained-1.1239963

6. Chilton, D. (1996). The wealthy barber: Everyone's common-sense guide to becoming financially independent. Rocklin, CA: Prima Pub.

7. Chilton, D. B. (2011). The wealthy barber returns: Significantly older and marginally wiser, Dave Chilton offers his unique perspectives on the world of money. Kitchener, Ont.: Financial Awareness.

8. CMHC - Buying a Home. (n.d.). Retrieved July 08, 2016, from https://www.cmhc-schl.gc.ca/en/co/buho/

9. Credit Score. (n.d.). Retrieved July 08, 2016, from http://www.ratehub.ca/credit-score

10. Debit Card vs Credit Card. (n.d.). Retrieved July 08, 2016, from http://www.diffen.com/difference/Credit_Card_vs_Debit_Card

11. El Issa, E. (2014, April 23). Will My Credit Score Follow Me If I Move to Another Country? - NerdWallet. Retrieved July 08, 2016, from https://www.nerdwallet.com/blog/credit-cards/credit-score-canad-move-expat-country-abroad/

12. Fisher, K. L., & Dellinger, E. (n.d.). Beat the crowd: How you can out-invest the herd by thinking differently.

13. Griffin, T. J. (2015). Charlie Munger the complete investor. New York, NY: Columbia Business School Publishing.

14. Khan, S. (n.d.). Annual percentage rate (APR) and effective APR. Retrieved July 08, 2016, from https://www.khanacademy.org/economics-finance-domain/core-finance/interest-tutorial/credit-card-interest/v/annual-percentage-rate-apr-and-effective-apr

15. Martin, F. (2013, July 3). Why the US bond market matters. Retrieved July 08, 2016, from http://www.newstatesman.com/business/2013/07/why-us-bond-market-matters-and-what-it-tells-us-about-world-economy

16. McInnes, M. (2007). Managing the law: The legal aspects of doing business. Toronto: Pearson Prentice Hall.

17. Median total income, by family type, by province and territory (All census families). (2015, June 26). Retrieved July 08, 2016, from http://www.statcan.gc.ca/tables-tableaux/sum-som/l01/cst01/famil108a-eng.htm

18. Mortgage-made-easy. Types of mortgages. (n.d.). Retrieved July 08, 2016, from http://www.mortgage-made-easy.com/types.htm

19. Mortgages 101: Buying your first home. (n.d.). Retrieved July

08, 2016, from http://www.fcac-acfc.gc.ca/Eng/forConsumers/topics/mortgages/Pages/Mortgage-Hypotheg.aspx

20. Types of Mortgages. (n.d.). Retrieved July 08, 2016, from http://www.mortgagebrokersottawa.com/mortgage-solutions/different-types-of-mortgages/

21. Pareto, C. (2015, December 16). Mutual Fund Or ETF: Which Is Right For You? | Investopedia. Retrieved July 08, 2016, from http://www.investopedia.com/articles/exchangetradedfunds/08/etf-mutual-fund-difference.asp

22. Patel, N. (2014, June 24). The Psychology of Instant Gratification and How It Will Revolutionize Your Marketing Approach. Retrieved July 08, 2016, from https://www.entrepreneur.com/article/235088

23. Press, K. (2015, March 18). How do employee pension plans work? Retrieved July 08, 2016, from https://www.sunlife.ca/ca/Learn and Plan/Money/Retirement savings/How do employee pension plans work?vgnLocale=en_CA

24. R., K. (2014, June 24). APR Explained. Retrieved July 8, 2016, from https://www.cashfloat.co.uk/apr-explained/

25. Satyanarayana, A. (2010, June 23). The Importance of Bond Markets and What They Mean To an Average Investor (J. C. Chavis, Ed.). Retrieved July 08, 2016, from http://www.brighthub.com/money/personal-finance/articles/13922.aspx

26. Schick, K. (2014, February 05). An Introduction To Stock Market Indexes | Investopedia. Retrieved July 08, 2016, from http://www.investopedia.com/articles/analyst/102501.asp

27. Stocks Basics: What Are Stocks? | Investopedia. (n.d.). Retrieved July 08, 2016, from http://www.investopedia.com/university/stocks/stocks1.asp

28. What Is a Bond? (n.d.). Retrieved July 08, 2016, from

http://guides.wsj.com/personal-finance/investing/what-is-a-bond/

29. Woodruff, M. (2016, May 5). 5 things I wish I knew before I got my first job. Retrieved July 8, 2016, from http://finance.yahoo.com/news/5-things-i-wish-i-knew-before-i-got-my-first-job-132512172.html

30. 10 Steps to Buying a House - Home Buying Process. (n.d.). Retrieved July 8, 2016, from https://www.discover.com/home-loans/articles/10-steps-to-buying-a-home

31. 10 steps of the homebuying process - Homeownership.ca. (2013). Retrieved July 8, 2016, from http://homeownership.ca/dreaming-of-homeownership/buy-vs-rent/ten-steps-of-the-homebuying-process/

Manufactured by Amazon.ca
Bolton, ON

28215641R00111